CAT & DOG PRAYER

D1166262

CAT & DOG PRAYER

RETHINKING OUR CONVERSATIONS WITH OUR MASTER

Bob Sjogren
and
Gerald Robison

IVP Books

An imprint of InterVarsity Press
Downers Grove, Illinois

InterVarsity Press
P.O. Box 1400, Downers Grove, IL 60515-1426
ivpress.com
email@ivpress.com

InterVarsity Press® is the book-publishing division of InterVarsity Christian Fellowship/USA®, a movement of students and faculty active on campus at hundreds of universities, colleges and schools of nursing in the United States of America, and a member movement of the International Fellowship of Evangelical Students. For information about local and regional activities, visit intervarsity.org.

Originally published by Biblica.

ISBN 978-0-8308-5620-6

Printed in the United States of America ⊛

Library of Congress Cataloging-in-Publication Data is available through the Library of Congress.

P	20	19	18	17	16	15	14	13	12	11	10	9	8	7	6	5
Y	30	29	28	27	26	25	24	23	22	21	20	19	18	17	16

To Frank and Ruth Osborne. Much of my life and ministry is the result of their prayers. They not only prayed for me but also provided me with my most-needed answer to prayer, their daughter as my wife!—Gerald

I write this in hopes that my children and those who read this will learn to pray effective kingdom prayers.—Bob

CONTENTS

INTRODUCTION

Prayer—It's Not about You

"It's not about you."[1]

The opening line of *The Purpose Driven Life* by Rick Warren has also been the essence of our *Cat and Dog Theology* book and seminars. Why is so much emphasis being given to this theme today? Because the church needs to hear it! The twenty-first-century church has been fed a diet of *me-ism*, a concept born in the sinful selfishness of the heart of humankind in the garden of Eden that's grown steadily ever since.

If we remember the proverb "Train up a child in the way he should go, and when he is old he will not turn from it" (Proverbs 22:6 NIV), it's easy to see how we got here. The church has existed more than two thousand years, yet in the last fifty years or so, our diet of strict me-ism has affected our attitudes, our way of life, our theology, and especially our prayers.

All Christians know they ought to pray. Almost all Christians do pray—sometimes. But there seems to be a problem with prayer. We don't find it seems to make a significant difference; that is, prayer doesn't seem to really work.

Why? Much of the answer lies in the fact that the hearts and minds of today's Christians have been steeped in Cat Theology. Let us remind you of the difference between Cat Theology and Dog Theology.

It's been said that dogs have masters and cats have staff. That is, dogs live to please their masters, while self-centered cats think their masters exist to please them. Cats and dogs see life from different vantage points and therefore come to two different conclusions about the same information.

Dogs look at all their masters do for them and think, *You feed me. You pet me. You shelter me. You love me. YOU MUST BE GOD!*

But cats look at the same information and think, *You feed me. You pet me. You shelter me. You love me. I MUST BE GOD!*

It's easy to see the difference. Cat Christians think everything is about them. They live at the center of their own universe. That's why UnveilinGLORY (the parent ministry of Cat and Dog Theology) has said we need a Copernican revolution in the church—we need to quit thinking everything revolves around us! Scripture is clear on this topic: "When you ask, you do not receive, because you ask with wrong motives, that you may spend what you get on your pleasures" (James 4:3 NIV).

The Bible tells us about people who prayed and the sun stood still, prayers that brought healing, caused rain in the midst of drought, overthrew armies, created an endless supply of oil, raised people from the dead, and Jesus even offered us ability to move mountains. But our reality is, we don't see mountains moving, we don't see the dead raised to life, there is no endless oil for us, no armies overthrown, no downpour of rain after a dry spell, the sick don't seem to be healed in any immediate fashion, and the earth doesn't stand still just because we pray that it will.

Yet it sounds heretical to say that prayer doesn't work. So what do we do?

Too often we live in a half-believing fantasy, a make-believe quasi world. We believe in our heart that our prayers do *something*, even though the real world doesn't seem to be moved by it. We feel guilty if we don't pray, but we often feel like helpless wimps when we do.

Yes, there is a problem with our prayers. But without a doubt the Bible teaches us to pray without a doubt, even though our experience seems to deny the teaching.

This book attempts to resolve some of this dilemma. We hope to give some direction and correction to our prayer lives, because often the problem with prayer is the *pray-er*.

- Sometimes the problem is our heart.
- Sometimes the problem is our intent.
- Sometimes the problem is our focus.
- Sometimes the problem is our thinking.
- Sometimes the problem is our wording.
- Sometimes the problem is our relationships.
- Sometimes the problem is our faith.

In other words, *we* are the problem with prayer. The problem is us.

Before we begin, we need to warn you: this is not a quick-fix book. There are no magic formulas or words that make prayer work. The truth is we *can't* make prayer work any more than we can make a river flow. God made rivers to flow, and He made prayer to work. We can only direct you to the river so you can get in it. We can only direct you to biblical prayer so you can get in its flow.

But much of the direction we will give is how to correct our focus on ourselves. Cats are praying about and for themselves and wondering why they don't get answers like the Dogs do. Perhaps what we're trying to say is that too often when we pray, all God hears is "MEow," when what moves Him to action is hearing a loud "BARK!" (Being All-Reliant on the King).

—The authors

1

The Problem of Prayer

One of the most disappointing and misunderstood aspects of the Christian life has to do with prayer. We're told that prayer is essential to the Christian life, that it is our main means of communication with God, and that it is our source of power for God's intervention in this life. We're told that God answers prayer and that our effectual prayers will be answered. In fact, we're told that if we ask *anything* in His name, He will do it.

But the sad fact is, most Christians are disappointed and frustrated, weak and ineffectual, ignorant and ignoring of their prayer lives. This raises a lot of questions:

- Why are so few prayers made?
- Why are so many prayers not answered?
- Are there different kinds of prayers?
- How are we to pray so that we do receive answers?
- Is there a secret to prayer?

Let's start with the basics. Prayer is nothing more than talking to God, having a conversation with Him just as you would with any other person. We're going to begin this book assuming a couple of things: first, that you are a Christian

(God does not obligate himself to answer any prayer of a unbeliever except the plea for salvation), and second, that you have already experienced prayer to some degree.

Now, what *type* of prayer have you used? Oops! You didn't know there were different kinds of prayer? Well, just as you have different kinds of conversations with people—so we do with God.

As we said, in its most basic form, prayer is simply communication with God. Sometimes we use prayer for praising Him, sometimes for confessing or asking forgiveness. In our most dire circumstances, we may use prayer to ask for deliverance. And of course we pray requesting wisdom or provision. Sometimes we want to plead and intervene for someone else; sometimes we just need to unload our thoughts and feelings.

But the prayers most often used, especially by Cat Christians, are those of *petition*, asking God to do something for us. We seem to have no hesitation about asking God to transcend heaven and earth, and time and space if necessary, for the purpose of changing some circumstance or giving us something we wouldn't get otherwise.

In this book we'll focus our attention on this prayer of petition. Why? Because this seems to be the area where we need the greatest help, guidance, and understanding.

Ready? Let's get started.

Why do Cat Christians find that their prayers of petition are so ineffective? Why aren't these prayers answered in more direct and obvious ways? A British Broadcasting Corporation online article titled "Does Prayer Work?" showed a picture of the pope and two other key Christian leaders. The caption read, "The world's religions got together a month ago to pray for peace. Has the planet seen any impact—and is there any evidence that praying works anyway?" The article elaborated:

> Just a month ago, the Pope led 200 religious leaders from round the world in prayers for peace.
>
> The venue for this landmark occasion was Assisi—the place which, fittingly, gave the world St Francis and his prayer "Make me a channel of your peace."
>
> And yet a month on, peace seems as elusive as ever. Dozens of Israelis and Palestinians have died. Worshippers at a Rawalpindi mosque have been gunned down. Fears of further conflict rose after President Bush spoke of an "axis of evil." Zimbabwe grows further from the world community. . . .
>
> [One] could scarcely conclude that prayers had been answered in any miraculous way.[2]

Why point out this article? Because it typifies Cat Christians' attitudes toward prayer: Why pray if my prayers aren't answered in any kind of miraculous way? Why pray if there's no obvious response from heaven? Why pray if there's no heavenly result? *Why bother?*

Good questions deserve good answers, so we're going to deal with this very problem.

The Bible records 161 prayers asking God to intervene. Ninety-eight received direct answers in the text. Take away the eleven that were answered with no, and that still leaves over a 50 percent rate of answered prayer. So why don't Cat Christians see that kind of response when they pray? Why don't they see the miraculous hand of God intervening in their affairs today?

One obvious answer is quite simple: they don't see God at work answering prayer because they don't pray very much.

Second, when they do ask, they have wrong motivations.

And third, Cats ask without consideration of what God wants, without caring about His purposes, and without insight and understanding as to what He might be doing.

We'll look at this third reason in more detail later in the book. For now, let's just briefly consider a biblical example of this—Peter's response to Jesus after Jesus had just described how He would need to go to Jerusalem and suffer: "Peter took Him aside and began to rebuke Him, saying, 'God forbid it, Lord! This shall never happen to You!'" (Matthew 16:22). As Cats do, Peter responded without understanding that this awful event that Jesus had just described was *in the will of God* and part of God's plan. That's why Jesus replied to Peter, "Get behind Me, Satan!" (v. 23).

How many times have we acted like Peter? We plead with God to do something or to keep something from happening without ever thinking that the very opposite of what we want might well be within God's plan. Not only that, but our own response might be just as far outside the will of God as we found the original set of circumstances to be.

Too Busy to Pray

Cat Christians say, "OK, so we don't pray much. But why should we if our prayers won't be answered?" We can ask the question in reverse: How can God answer a prayer that is never offered? If we took a poll around the nation and asked people, "How often do you pray?" or "How much time do you spend in prayer?" the answers might stun us.

When we asked that question on the internet, the most common answer we found was that on average, Christians pray between three and seven minutes per day, and much of that is in giving thanks for food. Pastors do only slightly better, with an average of five minutes a day. (Sounds pretty Catlike, doesn't it?)

Think about that for a moment. Why are we averaging only three minutes of prayer a day? The most common reason people give is that they are just *too busy*. If Cats do give God time, it's the scraps of the day.

We are so busy with life and work that there is very little time to be still and seek God. And because most parents don't pray, most kids follow suit. They don't pray because they don't see their parents praying. (Cats beget Cats.) Besides, kids are busy too. They've got school, extracurricular activities, and homework. They don't think there's time either.

God clearly explains to us, "You do not have, because you do not ask God" (James 4:2 NIV). Simply put, if we are not asking God to move, He won't.

Let's be honest here. If we prayed more, we would see more answers to our prayers! Maybe not as many as we'd like, but still a lot more. And *if we had evidence* that prayer really worked, wouldn't we make time — take time — and make it a much bigger part of our everyday routine? In fact, if we knew it really worked, wouldn't we schedule the rest of our day around our prayer time?

We Want What We Want — But We Don't Have Many Needs

There's another reason why Cats don't pray much. It's not

just busyness that keeps them from praying. Most people in North America have very few physical needs.

Most of us are rich by comparison with the rest of the world. So why should we go to the Lord and say, "Give us this day our daily bread" when all we have to do is go to the store and buy it? For real needs, we've been trained to look elsewhere, whether it's the government, the bank, or our credit card companies. Most of us tend to look there first and go to God in prayer only when nothing else works.

But much of the world lives far differently than we do. As you read this, there are moms and dads in other parts of the world who get up each morning not knowing where they will find food for their family. If they are praying, trust us—it's for more than our average three minutes a day! Many undoubtedly practice prayer without ceasing. Their hungry stomachs are their constant reminder to trust in the provision of the Lord.

Without a need, we seem to have little motivation for prayer. In our three minutes a day, as long as no crisis or catastrophe has come our way, we can stop in to check up on God and let Him know we're thinking of Him and doing our daily homage.

Wants or Needs?

Parents are all too familiar with their children's nagging requests for the latest toys, clothes, or whatever is popular at the moment. After all, they "need" it! (At least, that's what we're told.) Being loving parents, we often fulfill these pleas, only to find the must-have thing discarded soon after purchase. What our children "needed" wasn't needed at all; it was only wanted, and it satisfied only temporarily.

Gerald's mother had a saying that might describe most

Cat Christians. It went like this: "I want what I want when I want it. When I've got what I want, I don't want what I've got. So I didn't really want what I wanted when I wanted it." That pretty accurately depicts the prayers of Cats too. They are looking for some immediate want to be met, not knowing that it isn't what they really need and that it won't satisfy for long.

Often we don't even go to God with our wants. Instead, we look for self-arranged means of providing ourselves with what we desire. To get our wants met in our culture, we go to our creditors more often than we go to our God.

So should we start praying for those extras in life, asking God to provide them instead of working for them? Will that bring about more direct answers to our prayers?

Not necessarily. Often, getting a positive answer to our request for God to provide depends not only on *what* we are praying for but *why* we are asking for it.

The Motive behind Our Requests

Prayers in the Bible for oneself are not necessarily self-ish or self-centered. Many are for deep concerns and critical needs, such as safety, wisdom, and physical provision. But this is quite the opposite of what we usually hear today. What we face isn't much different from what James expressed when he chastised: "When you ask, you do not receive, because you ask with wrong motives, that you may spend what you get on your pleasures" (James 4:3 NIV). The verb *ask* is in the middle voice of the Greek language, meaning "ask for yourself." In other words, we're greedy and selfish in our prayers, so despite the time and attention we give to prayer, we are not rewarded for it.

Indeed, in the language James used, the word *spend* might be better translated "squander." And the word for *pleasures* is the word from which we derive *hedonism* and *hedonistic*. A Cat Christian's prayers can be aptly described as hedonistic squandering.

What James was saying is this: "God should not be expected to provide for hedonistic squandering. Therefore, your prayers are not being answered because you keep praying self-centered, selfish prayers."

Some Cat Christians are being taught to ask God for *anything* they want without consideration of God's will or how their selfish squandering might affect others. They are being told this kind of prayer is within their rights as children of God, and testimonies abound about how God has poured out abundant blessings on this kind of prayer.

And even though God warns us against praying this way, we still do. Why? Because we are steeped in Cat Theology.

The War of Two Natures

The Bible speaks of believers as having two natures. There is the old nature that Paul called "hostile toward God" and "fleshly" (Romans 8:7; 1 Corinthians 3:3)—we call this being a Cat. It is the natural person inside you without Christ. It's also called the earthly nature or human nature. In its purest form it is ugly, egotistical, and selfish and lives for itself. By its nature it does things that are pleasing to itself rather than pleasing to God.

On the other hand, when a person becomes a Christian, he or she is a "new creature" (2 Corinthians 5:17); that is, a person with a new nature. Just as a father's seed implanted into a woman produces a baby, so God, by the Holy Spirit, enters us and brings new birth. That's why Christians are called born again.

Unfortunately, this new nature doesn't arrive fully mature, and neither does it totally displace the old nature. We are left with two warring natures inside of us. We notice this internal conflict when we don't do what is right and choose to do what we know is wrong. Paul described it this way: "For what I am doing, I do not understand; for I am not practicing what I would like to do, but I am doing the very thing I hate" (Romans 7:15). The Bible further illustrates this when it declares, "Those who belong to Christ Jesus have crucified the flesh with its passions and desires" (Galatians 5:24). Yet it also says that we are to put to death whatever belongs to the old nature (Colossians 3:5). How can we put it to death unless it is still alive in us? And how can it be alive in us if it was crucified? How can both statements be true?

When the Bible speaks of the crucifixion of our old nature, it means that the old nature is no longer the sole authority and decision maker in our life. Before we came to know Christ, sin controlled us completely—similar to how unrestrained wild animals behave, we did whatever sin led us to do without thinking twice.

But now as believers with a new nature, we are united with the Holy Spirit, who will lead us into truth and let us know when we are straying away from the will of our Father. We can allow this new nature to control us, and when we do, the old nature takes a back seat.

Again, Galatians 5 speaks of this situation: "But I say, walk by the Spirit, and you will not carry out the desire of the flesh. For the flesh sets its desire against the Spirit, and the Spirit against the flesh" (vv. 16–17). These two natures conflict with one another. They battle for control. Which one you allow to win the battle determines whether you are living your life by God's power or by your own power. This war inside us can be described as us fighting against ourselves, and we're fighting like Cats and Dogs!

What Paul described is like the children's game King of the Hill. In this game one person stands on top of a mound, proclaiming to be king of the hill. Then all the other players struggle to dethrone that person and proclaim themselves king instead. This is a great picture of our two natures warring inside us. This is why Paul said, "But if you are led by the Spirit, you are not under the Law" (v. 18).

It's clear that the Bible recognizes the pains we go through in our decision-making process, even when we are deciding what to pray. Yes, we can pray selfishly, squandering the opportunity by praying for worldly desires, and that is why so many prayers are not answered. Even though by praying we seem to be focused and dependent on God, our old nature turns our time with God into a time to focus God's attention, care, and power toward *ourselves*! Cats ask, "What can I get God to do for me? What can I ask God to get for me? How can God make my life safer, softer, easier, and more comfortable?"

Perhaps you've heard the story of two dogs in a fight. They are equal in size and tenacity. The question is, Which dog will win the fight? The answer is, The one you feed the most. So which of your two natures will win the fight in your prayer life, the old worldly nature or the new holy nature? The one you feed the most.

The theological word *sanctified* describes something that is set apart or holy. God has set us apart for himself, and He wants us to set ourselves apart from worldly desires.

Sanctification is the process of being made more and more holy (Christlike) by allowing more and more of the new nature to control our life, thoughts, prayers, and decisions. But our North American culture is geared toward feeding our old selfish nature. Nearly all advertising is purposed to make us want something we don't have, and it works very, very well. Subconsciously, we feed our old nature by exposing it to worldly stimulation and a daily regimen of me-ism. Our new nature starves.

As a result, our prayers become more and more focused on ourselves, our desires, and our plans rather than on God's. Our prayers have a lot of *I*, *me*, and *my* in them. As James described, we end up praying for hedonistic squandering, and God does not answer.

What did we learn in this chapter?
We learned that too many prayers of petition and intercession are not being answered for one of two Cat reasons: first, Cats are not praying much, and second, Cats are praying selfishly.

2

Cats and Dogs Examine the Model Prayer

In chapter 1 we found that Cat Christians don't pray much, or if they do, their prayers are short and selfish (the very definition of Cat Prayer). God doesn't answer unprayed prayers or prayers for what will be selfishly squandered. Because those are the prayers Cats most often pray, they're left thinking God doesn't answer prayer—that prayer doesn't really work.

In this book we're trying to give prayer a second chance, to learn how to pray prayers that *do* get answered—how to move from Cat Prayer to Dog Prayer.

But trust us, Dog Christians have no secret password, no abracadabra, no special phrase, no secret button. If that's what you're looking for, you won't find it here—or anywhere else. (In spite of hearing this, Cat Christians will keep on hoping and searching for the prayer shortcuts that will get them what they want.)

So what does make our prayers more effective? The disciples had the same question, and they said to Jesus, "Lord, teach us to pray" (Luke 11:1). Remember that God invites us to talk to Him, and He not only gives us this privilege but He commands that we pray. He promises to answer prayer. If He doesn't, it's our fault, not His.

When Jesus taught the disciples (and us) to pray, He didn't pass along secret words, a pass code, or a secret combination to God's "prayer safe." Instead, He gave us a model, or pattern, and said to follow it as an example. Note that He didn't say to pray these exact *words*; He said, "Pray, then, in this way" (Matthew 6:9). He said, in essence, something like this: "If you want effective, effectual prayers, these are the topics or principles that I want you to base your prayers on. If you do, your prayers will be pleasing to the Father."

About now, both Cats and Dogs are eager to read on— Cats so they can persuade God to give them something they want for themselves and Dogs so they can be used by God for His purposes. As we examine Jesus' prayer pattern, sometimes called the model prayer (Matthew 6:9–13), we'll find an answer for ourselves too. Here we'll do a "prayer-a-phrase"— we'll look at the prayer phrase by phrase to discover Jesus' template for effective prayer. The model prayer begins, "Our Father who is in heaven."

"Our Father Who Is in Heaven"

First and foremost, Dogs begin by recognizing that they direct their prayers to God, who desires a closer relationship with us. We come to Him and relate to Him as our Father. Just as children are dependent on their fathers, so we are to be absolutely dependent on our heavenly Father. It is God alone to whom we pray and whom we depend on. He loves us, his children, just as an earthly father should love his kids. He provides for us, just as an earthly father should. He wants to teach us, train us, and help us mature, just as an earthly father should. This is a love connection rather than a distant relationship.

Dogs realize that if God doesn't act, nothing will happen. Without Him their prayers will not be answered despite anything they do!

As I (Bob) type these words, I'm sitting in an airport in New York, snowed in, trying to get home; my seminar was cancelled. I'm supposed to go overseas next week, but there are problems with my visa. I've done everything I can; I've called, questioned, argued, and gotten frustrated and stressed. My wife has suffered the same. Even at this stage of my Christian life, I have to pause, remember, and renew my relationship with my Father. I cannot control the weather—He can. I can't do anything more about my visa—He can. And even now I'm relearning to rest in Him, to depend totally on Him.

Now let's move on to the second phrase of the model prayer.

"Hallowed Be Your Name"

To hallow means "to venerate, to regard as holy, to consider as sacred." This reminds Dogs that everything is to revolve around God, for He alone is holy and sacred. He is to be exalted. His name is to be lifted high above all others. In the context of a father-child relationship, again, this is a love connection. We venerate God's name and praise Him because we admire, respect, and stand in awe of Him—not merely because He is omnipotent (having unlimited authority) but because we love Him.

Let's put these first two phrases together: "Our Father

who is in heaven, hallowed be Your name." Dogs learn to begin their prayers with praise and adoration for who God is and their relationship with Him. Dogs honor God, praising Him for His magnificence and adoring Him for what He represents. And this God, who is so magnificent, so awesome, is to be recognized as a father—our Father. By coming to Him as our Father, we also recognize our dependence on Him and our relationship with Him.

In the age in which we live, we far too often rely on ourselves, our abilities, our attempts, our contacts. If all of these fail, *then* we pray. It seems that no matter how often a pastor teaches this, God is able to make us learn it again. (I'm still in the snowbound airport!)

"Your Kingdom Come"

Dogs recognize that God is not only our Father but also a king. And not just *a* king or *our* king but the King of Kings! As a king, He has a kingdom. And if Dogs ask that His kingdom come, they must be in agreement with it. They must desire it and be in alignment with it. Their thoughts, their patriotism, their allegiance must be with that kingdom.

Before we pray, "Your kingdom come," a good old-fashioned self-examination is in order. Are we committed to God's kingdom? Is it our greatest desire? Is our allegiance with its values? Just repeating the words by rote memory is no use. Saying the words doesn't mean we are committed to their meaning.

Isaiah once spoke of God this way: "Your name and renown are the desire of our hearts" (Isaiah 26:8 NIV). Could you honestly say that? Does your heart and soul long for Him to be king? Your king? Your King of Kings? Is the establishment of

His kingdom your great desire and something you would die for? Just as important—maybe more so—is whether God's kingdom is what you live for.

Cat Christians say yes to these questions easily, and they might even mean what they say. However, for me (Gerald) the words haven't always come from my heart but from my head. I knew I was supposed to say these words and I was supposed to mean them. And maybe I did mean them, but not at the heart level.

Really wanting this at the heart level may mean Cats need to learn to fall in love with God all over again.

"Your Will Be Done, on Earth as It Is in Heaven"

A king has subjects, loyal followers who have pledged their allegiance to him. This is what Jesus was really speaking of in the next phrase of the model prayer. This is about more than recognition of God's kingship. Jesus was speaking of *lordship*, a willing and desirous submission to Him.

Acknowledging a desire for God's lordship is one thing; submission to it is something else. For example, being a member of a political party and considering yourself committed to it doesn't mean you give total submission to the party's desires. Your vote might fall in line with the party platform, and you might desire for that party to lead the government, but if you were called for financial support, you probably wouldn't say, "Just tell me how much—I'll give whatever you say!" There is a very big difference between support and obedience.

With that insight, you can better understand this line of Jesus' model prayer. Dogs recognize this line as complete and willing submission. *Your kingdom come!*

"Give Us This Day Our Daily Bread"

At this point, the focus moves from God to us. When Cat Christians near this part of the prayer, they might be tempted to think, *Is this where we get to tell Him all the things we want?*

Note that the prayer is nearly halfway completed before our needs, our desires, and our personal agenda are even mentioned. Even an *intercessory* prayer (a prayer for someone or something other than ourselves) begins with recognition of who God is, His rightful place, and our willing submission to Him *before* we venture our request.

The change of subject from God establishing His kingdom on earth to meeting our daily needs is not a hyperjump. Jesus does not have attention deficit disorder. He's not randomly changing topics. There is a link between the establishment of God's kingdom and our being in daily submission and dependency on Him.

Gerald's wife, Sharon, is prone to begin a conversation when she's already in the middle of a thought. To Gerald the conversation seems to begin out of nowhere and can change course at any moment. We've decided Sharon doesn't have a "train of thought" but bumper cars! The model prayer isn't like that. Jesus wasn't abruptly changing topics. The advancement of God's kingdom here on earth inherently involves both the recruitment and sustaining of His people. Only as God supplies our elemental needs can we advance His kingdom.

Bob's family has a friend named Brianna with some health challenges at this time in her life. She needs to be extremely careful about what she eats or else she becomes sick quickly and has no energy to do anything. Before, prayers for her usually went something like this: "Lord, heal Brianna so she can have strength and energy, so she can live a full, energetic life without such a handicap." Our thought was that surely God can heal her and wants to heal her so she can live normally. But the prayer fell short because it was never linked to God's kingdom. Yes, we were interceding for Brianna. Yes, we were letting our requests be made known. And yes, maybe this was even a daily dependency on God. But something was missing—that link to God's purposes and God's kingdom.

Today our prayers for Brianna are different. Now we make the connection to the kingdom: "Lord, Brianna is a subject within your kingdom, and you've purposed her to assist in the establishment of it. But how can she be thoroughly involved and actively participating when she is sick and has no energy? For the sake of your great and holy name, for the sake of her help in establishing your kingdom, we ask that you heal her so she can work to make you famous."

In our previous book, *Cat and Dog Theology*, Gerald related how he had to learn this lesson in a most unusual circumstance. Gerald took his little dog for a walk. Wanting to hurry home and not miss the beginning of a television show, he kept encouraging the dog to go ahead and "do its thing." But the dog was having trouble; its bodily systems weren't in sync with Gerald's expectations. The dog would walk, stop, squat . . . nothing. They'd walk further, and the dog would stop, squat . . . nothing. In a moment of exasperation, Gerald mumbled, "God, would you make the dog poop so I can watch my show!"

That's when it occurred to him how ludicrous and self-centered his prayer was. He was asking God to transcend time and space, to interrupt the normal and regular functions of this world to let his dog poop so he could watch television.

That was when Gerald decided to let God teach him to pray. After considerable thought, introspection, and consideration, Gerald prayed this way: "God, you've made a beautifully starry night, the clouds are translucent, and the mood is gorgeous. As people, we are truly fearfully and wonderfully made. All creation radiates your glory through the things you've made. But Father, tonight your design, your creativity, and your glory aren't showing through this little dog. His body isn't reflecting the glory you put there; it's just not functioning the way you designed. For your glory, so the dog radiates your handiwork and your kingdom, would you fix its systems?"

The dog pooped. Gerald went home and to this day doesn't remember watching television, but he does remember the night he finally learned to pray with God and His kingdom in mind.

Admittedly, some might find this illustration a bit boorish or crude. Sorry about that! But God can use any circumstance to teach us important things. The lesson to learn is how to connect our prayers to God's kingdom.

So what kinds of things *should* we be asking for? Both Cats and Dogs want to know.

Well, Jesus' example is worth an examination. What did He say to ask for? Our "daily bread."

Now, some might inquire, "Daily bread? But what about the car, the house, the extra things I've been wanting? After all, what about *me*?" Well, if we're honest about what we see in this prayer, no extras are mentioned—only needs. Cats are sorely disappointed by this.

And notice that the need is for daily provision—just like the manna God provided the Israelites in the Old Testament. If they gathered more than they needed for one day, the remainder became rancid (Exodus 16:16–20). God provided manna on a daily basis for the purpose of his children recognizing daily dependence on Him as their sole provider. If they could have stockpiled the manna, they wouldn't have felt an immediate need for God's provision. In this same way, Christ pointed us to "daily bread"—a daily dependence on God for the very necessities of life. This is not about seeking our desires, wants, and wish lists or our long-term goals and dreams. Jesus pointed us to dependency—total, daily, full, absolute dependency on God. This is about asking for essential things, those things that if we don't get them, we die.

Cats have a tendency to give little heed to this part of the prayer, as we mentioned in chapter 1, because most of their essential needs are covered on a day-to-day basis. There are few things they can't save, store up, or hoard.

This part of the prayer is almost lost on us because we so rarely face a situation in which we need God on a daily basis for the basics of life-sustaining elements. Bread? We just go to the store and buy it. With preservatives and the abundance available to us, we certainly don't need to go daily. So why would we need to pray for something so readily available and easy to obtain? The answer is that without daily recognition of our total dependence on God, we are apt to believe that we obtained what we have without Him.

This is not an unusual circumstance for humanity or a surprise to God. He even warned the Israelites about this before they went into the Promised Land:

> When the LORD your God brings you into the land which He swore to your fathers, Abraham, Isaac and Jacob, to give you, great

> and splendid cities which you did not build, and houses full of all good things which you did not fill, and hewn cisterns which you did not dig, vineyards and olive trees which you did not plant, and you eat and are satisfied, then watch yourself, that you do not forget the LORD. . . .
>
> Beware that you do not forget the LORD your God by not keeping His commandments and His ordinances and His statutes which I am commanding you today; otherwise, when you have eaten and are satisfied, and have built good houses and lived in them, and when your herds and your flocks multiply, and your silver and gold multiply, and all that you have multiplies, then your heart will become proud and you will forget the LORD your God. (Deuteronomy 6:10–12; 8:11–14)

This is a constant and inherent danger in the minds and hearts of Cats, and it has incalculable repercussions and consequences in their relationship with God.

When we realize the asking-for-us part of the model prayer and the recognizing-God part are linked, we should question our motivation for every prayer. We should be examining our prayer requests based on these considerations:

- Is this request a need?
- Is this request showing my dependency on God?
- Is this request linked to the establishment of God's kingdom?

When this examination of your prayers and your heart

becomes a regular part of your prayer life—you're going to find your prayers becoming more and more effective and powerful and answered more and more often. Congratulations! You're learning to bark!

Next, Jesus' model prayer moves on to forgiveness.

"Forgive Us Our Debts, as We Also Have Forgiven Our Debtors"

The translation I (Gerald) remember used the word "trespasses" instead of "debts." It implied that I had stepped beyond a permissible border with someone else. If I have violated a personal boundary with someone—if I have "gone too far" and brought hurt, pain, ridicule, lack of respect, or unwarranted trouble to another—it will, in turn, interfere with my relationship with God.

Trespasses in our relationships with others (being "indebted" to them) disrupts our relationship with God. One glaring example in Scripture says, "Husbands, in the same way be considerate as you live with your wives, and treat them with respect . . . *so that nothing will hinder your prayers*" (1 Peter 3:7 NIV, emphasis added).

How many prayers are not being answered because of poor relationships between husbands and wives? How many men are discouraged by their lack of answered prayers without understanding that it may be the result of their own doing?

Listen to this: relationships count! Mark it down. Remember it. Engrave it on your heart! Relationships with God and with people interconnect, intertwine, and interfere with one another. Your auto mechanic knows that a problem with your automobile may be the symptom from any number of sources. In the same way, a malfunction in our spiritual life can be a symptom of a problem in our relationships.

Men, your relationship with God is somewhat determined by your relationship with your wife . . . but certainly, not just with your wife—it's ALL your relationships because each person is created in the image of God and deserves respect. If we can't respect those who are made in His image, how can He expect us to respect Him? And how can we hope for some favorable answer to our prayers? Unanswered prayers may be due to unattended or overlooked connections with your spouse. Correct one and you might correct the other.

"And Do Not Lead Us into Temptation, but Deliver Us from Evil"

It seems that Cats' natural curiosity often draws them into dangerous territory. This portion of the model prayer asks God to keep us safe and usable for His kingdom and the purpose for which He created us, to bring Him glory—a plea for God to keep us safe from ourselves and from the evil one who stalks us. The Bible describes Satan as a "roaring lion, seeking someone to devour" (1 Peter 5:8).

When I (Gerald) was a child, the men and boys in our church went on a boat trip down a Florida river inhabited by alligators. The men chose an island as a place to camp that night, and I remember my dad putting me in the bow of our boat and telling me to go to sleep. But shortly after saying our good-nights, I heard men yelling warnings to each other along with the sound of something big splashing the water near the side of our boat. I jumped up, yelling to know what was happening but was told, "We just caught an alligator—go back to sleep."

Go back to sleep? Are you kidding me? There's a gator

outside the boat! Yet my father said those words that many fathers have repeated throughout the years: "It's OK. I'm right here!" And with those words I was comforted enough that I was able to get back to sleep. Why? Because I knew my father loved me and would watch out for me. He would either keep the gators from me or me from the gators.

This part of Jesus' prayer pattern isn't much different. It's a plea for our heavenly Father—who never slumbers or sleeps—to watch over us and keep us from evil. With this comes the realization that if the devil does affect us, it's with our Father's permission and with His good goal in mind. Paul realized this when he had prayed three times for God to change his circumstances:

> To keep me from exalting myself, there was given me a thorn in the flesh, a messenger of Satan to torment me—to keep me from exalting myself! Concerning this I implored the Lord three times that it might leave me. And He has said to me, "My grace is sufficient for you, for power is perfected in weakness." Most gladly, therefore, I will rather boast about my weaknesses, so that the power of Christ may dwell in me. Therefore I am well content with weaknesses, with insults, with distresses, with persecutions, with difficulties, for Christ's sake; for when I am weak, then I am strong. (2 Corinthians 12:7–10)

Here was an occasion in which Paul's prayer was *not* answered the way he wanted, but Paul found solace in the "no" he did receive. There's a lesson for us too—actually, there are several:

- We are to take our plea to God.
- Sometimes evil does touch us, in spite of our prayers.
- When that happens, it doesn't mean God didn't answer; it means He had another plan and He is still lovingly involved.
- When God has another plan, we need to learn to flow with it.

Notice Paul's response to his situation—it isn't one of huge disappointment, frustration, and exasperation with God. Instead, Paul found God's purpose and his place in God's good will. He even found contentment (v. 10) in this unsought situation, so that Christ's power would dwell in him. Cats find it nearly impossible to have this attitude.

Learning to go with the flow is more easily said than done, but it's more easily done when we find ourselves totally dependent and trusting in Him who holds all the possibilities in His all-powerful hand.

Realize this: you are a target of Satan. Why? Because if he can destroy, detain, and detour your advancement of God's kingdom, he wins an advantage. He wants to ruin your life so that God is robbed of His glory. As a result, you're not going to get through this life unscathed, unhurt, or untouched. You may face tragedy, calamity, distress, adversity, persecution, weakness, and more. That doesn't mean God isn't answering your prayer.

God's purpose might not be that our life is safe, soft, easy, and comfortable—the dream and request of most Cat Christians. Dog Christians understand this and willingly, lovingly, totally, wholeheartedly, and submissively place themselves in God's hands, at God's disposal, for God's purpose.

"For Yours Is the Kingdom and the Power and the Glory Forever"

Finally, we come to the last line in Jesus' model prayer. (Many translations of the Bible place this line in a footnote.)

The pattern of prayer Jesus gave us both starts and ends with worship. Paul also understood that everything is from God, through Him, and to Him.

It's our desire that in this chapter you have begun to see the differences in how Jesus taught us to pray and how Cats tend to pray. Jesus' prayer was God centered and God focused. The prayers James warned about are us centered and us focused and, as he described it, filled with hedonistic squandering. In self-centered prayers, God might hear nothing more than "Meow, meow, meow."

What did we learn in this chapter?

We looked at the prayer model Jesus gave His disciples when they asked Him to teach them to pray. The model prayer is a pattern, or template, for prayer—not magical words and not a secret password or special key to pick the lock of God's "prayer box."

The pattern shows us that prayer is intricately wrapped up in God, not us. Prayer is given to strengthen both our relationship with God *and* our dependency on Him. The prayer pattern Jesus us gave links our needs to God's purposes, His being, and His kingdom.

3

Learning to Ask Big

Let's suppose you need a new car, but you don't have the money or credit to buy one. So you come to one of us and ask if we will help you. Being the generous people we are, we say, "Anything we have is yours," and we hand you a blank check. We've signed it, and you can write in whatever amount you need.

Let's keep supposing that the car you want costs twenty thousand dollars, so you write in that amount, but when you take the check to the bank, the teller says, "Sorry, that check is no good. The account doesn't have sufficient funds to cover it."

Now let's pretend that the check is signed not by us but by Bill and Melinda Gates—and you don't know who they are. But this time when you take the check to the bank, you have no problems at all. The check is good, the teller hands you the cash you need, and you are thoroughly satisfied and happy—*until* you discover the identities of Bill and Melinda Gates! When you realize they are among the wealthiest people who have ever lived and you could have written that check for a much, *much*, *MUCH* larger amount, you don't feel quite as happy as you did before. Now you realize how much more you could have had. Your use of the blank check didn't even come close to its full potential.

Now let's pretend one more time. This time, instead of a check signed by us or Bill and Melinda Gates, it is signed by Jesus. He's waiting for you to fill in your name and what you want. What will you write?

This is not just a rhetorical or theoretical question. Let's look at the words of Jesus to His disciples: "Whatever you ask in My name, that will I do" (John 14:13).

Are we to take this literally?

You have your doubts, but then Jesus repeats his statement: "Truly, truly, I say to you, if you ask the Father for anything in My name, He will give it to you. Until now you have asked for nothing in My name; ask and you will receive" (John 16:23–24).

Notice that Jesus didn't begin with, "Rhetorically and theoretically, I say to you." He said, "Truly, truly." This is *truth*.

Why did Jesus say "Truly, truly" when just one *truly* would have sufficed? The Jews repeated words in order to emphasize them. You and I might *italicize* a word, write it in CAPITAL LETTERS, or put it in **bold print**, but the Jews would repeat it. Jesus was saying, "What I'm telling you is really, really ***TRUE***!"

Cat Christians are puzzled at this point. They want their prayers answered. After all, there's so much to get in order to make their lives safer, softer, easier, and a little more comfortable. So they wonder, Can we really ask Him for all the things we've been dreaming of—cars, a bigger home, a second home, a lavish and opulent lifestyle . . . and more? Are the prosperity-teaching preachers teaching truth after all?

Before we fill in the blank on this check, we must go back and realize once again why James 4:3 tells us our prayers aren't being answered—because we ask motivated by hedonistic squandering! "You ask and do not receive, because you ask with wrong motives, so that you may spend it on your pleasures." (I'm guessing James was aiming this comment directly at the Cats.)

Praying in Jesus' Name

Notice that Jesus said we can ask for anything in His name. That does not mean we create our wish list, present it to Him, and then add, "In Jesus' name. Amen." If that were true, then "in Jesus' name" would be nothing more than magical words tacked on to the end of our prayers, nothing more than abracadabra.

So before we can ask God for "anything," we need to understand what it means to pray in Jesus' name, and Dog Christians have done exactly that. How do they know those words aren't a magical incantation? They know because of the example left us by the very disciples of Jesus. Throughout the New Testament *not one* prayer ends "in Jesus' name."

Doesn't that strike you as somewhat amazing? For nearly fifty years I've heard prayers all over the globe closed with those endearing words—yet not one biblical character closed a prayer that way. This clearly shows Dogs these words alone are not the key to answered prayer—or even to spiritually minded prayer. The effectual part of the prayer is not the abracadabra of "in Jesus' name" but rather the spirit, heart, motivation, and consideration of the prayer.

So what does it mean to ask in Jesus' name?

In the Bible a person's name often tells us something about his or her character or reputation. *Jacob* means "deceiver." *Abraham* means "father of many nations." *Immanuel* means "God with us." A person's name can represent something about his personality, his origin, or sometimes even his destiny. This is why young boys are often instructed by their fathers to be careful so as not to destroy their good name.

When Dogs pray in Jesus' name, they're saying, "Lord, what I'm asking for is consistent with your character, your personality, your purposes, your plans, and destiny for creation." Before we utter any words in prayer, we should be making absolutely certain that our request is in alignment with God's will and purposes. We might be considering in pre-prayer time what God wants us to do in this situation. How would Jesus be praying this prayer? I want what Jesus wants—not what my carnal, natural, selfish nature might want to ask. If God's kingdom is to be established, what should I be praying to make that happen? When we begin to pray this way and with this consideration, we can say that we have been praying in the name of Jesus—the Dogs are learning to bark!

In the previous chapter, we saw a hint of this in the model prayer with its use of "Hallowed be Your name," an expression and desire for God's name to be lifted up and exalted. So anything prayed in Jesus' name should be in alignment with His character and personality—as if He himself were making the request. In other words, if Jesus wouldn't make a particular request, neither should we. This should cause us to question and evaluate the motivations for our prayer. *Why* are we praying this? For our kingdom or for His kingdom?

If Jesus' signature is on the check, we must be certain the request is one He would sign.

Praying with God's Kingdom in Mind

Let's examine two prayers found in the Bible. Both were answered in a positive way. Let's check the motivation for each prayer.

The first is found in the book of Joshua. Joshua had just crossed the Jordan River with the Israelites and was leading them into the Promised Land. After victory at Jericho came the people's first loss, at Ai. When Joshua's men returned in defeat, Joshua prayed, "O Lord GOD, why did You ever bring this people over the Jordan, only to deliver us into the hand of the Amorites, to destroy us?" (Joshua 7:7).

So far the prayer certainly seems centered on Joshua and his people, but as we look further, we find this: "If only we had been willing to dwell beyond the Jordan! O Lord, what can I say since Israel has turned their back before their enemies? For the Canaanites and all the inhabitants of the land will hear of it, and they will surround us and cut off our name from the earth" (vv. 7–9). That still sounds as if Joshua is meowing in a self-centered way. He is worried about "our name" (referring to the Israelites) being cut off from the earth.

But as we look to the end of verse 9, we see the name of the people intrinsically linked to the name and reputation of God: "For the Canaanites and all the inhabitants of the land will hear of it, and they will surround us and cut off our name from the earth. *And what will You do for Your great name?*" (v. 9, emphasis added). In other words, Joshua said, "Lord, if we are destroyed, how can we serve you and advance your kingdom? This is about you, Lord. Don't let this happen!" (This sounds like barking to us!)

While Joshua's prayer was for the future of his people, it was ultimately for—and based on—the reputation and name of God himself. This is exactly how we were taught to pray in the pattern Jesus gave us. Praying for our needs isn't wrong, but we need to pray about them in the context of God's kingdom. Cat prayers aren't necessarily wrong, just incomplete or prayed with wrong priorities.

The second prayer we want to examine is found in the book of Daniel. The Israelites had been conquered by other nations as a consequence of their sins. At the time of this prayer, they were in captivity in Babylon, and the city of Jerusalem—including the temple—lay in ruins. Daniel was one of those taken captive to Babylon, where he prayed (he barked!) for the restoration of God's people to their homeland.

Just as we were taught to pray, Daniel began his prayer with praise: "Now, O Lord our God, who have brought Your people out of Egypt with a mighty hand and have made a name for Yourself, as it is this day" (Daniel 9:15). Then followed a confession of sin: "We have sinned, we have been wicked. O Lord, in accordance with all Your righteous acts, let now Your anger and Your wrath turn away from Your city Jerusalem, Your holy mountain; for because of our sins and the iniquities of our fathers, Jerusalem and Your people have become a reproach to all those around us" (vv. 15–16).

Daniel then asked God to act: "So now, our God, listen to the prayer of Your servant and to his supplications, and for Your sake, O Lord, let Your face shine on Your desolate sanctuary" (v. 17).

Did you notice the word *reproach* in verse 16? It sounds harsh . . . and it was. Daniel told God what others were saying about His people, and then he connected that to God's name. Herein is the powerful source of Daniel's prayer: *the prayer was about God*, not just His people. Daniel pleaded with God,

"For Your sake, O Lord." And hear how he continued in verse 18: "O my God, incline Your ear and hear! Open Your eyes and see our desolations and the city which is called by Your name; for we are not presenting our supplications before You on account of any merits of our own, but on account of Your great compassion."

God is not drawn to action based on our righteousness or our great merit. He is drawn for His own name's sake and out of mercy and grace for us who are not worthy. If God were to act based on what we deserve, we would get only death and damnation in hell, because that is exactly what our ongoing sins justly deserve.

Daniel ended his prayer with these words: "O Lord, hear! O Lord, forgive! O Lord, listen and take action! For Your own sake, O my God, do not delay, because Your city and Your people are called by Your name" (v. 19). Here we see that the last words of Daniel's request were about God—God's name and God's glory. Over and over again, Daniel prayed for God's intervention *based on the connection between the situation of God's people and God's reputation.*

These two prayers of Joshua and Daniel came at critical times in the history of God's people. Joshua and Daniel might naturally have meowed only "God, help us!" But both men resisted that urge and barked their causes based on God's name and reputation, not their own. Joshua and Daniel both had the opportunity to fill in a blank check, and they filled it in with what was in line with God's character and concern. One asked for deliverance for an entire nation, and the other asked for the rebuilding of an entire nation. Their concerns were *big*, their foundation was strong, and their prayers were answered.

God has perfect timing. As I (Bob) worked on this chapter,

a couple very close to my family experienced terrible marriage problems and looked to us for help. Because I love them so much, I wanted to cry out to God, "For their sake, O Lord, please heal their marriage." And while I could have prayed this prayer passionately, it would not have been an effectual and powerful prayer. (Cat prayers can sound more spiritually inclined than they are if they are passionately prayed.)

I had to resist praying the way that seemed so natural. I realized that praying "for their sake" should not be my primary motivation. It's not a bad motivation, but it's not the best. I needed to pray as one seeking to establish God's kingdom, as one thoroughly concerned with God's reputation. I had to learn how to pray all over again. I needed to pray for His name's sake. So how did I pray?

> God, how can they focus on your kingdom when their marriage is in such bad shape? How can they tell others about you and represent you when their lives are filled with such pain? How can their marriage be compared to your relationship with us when they can't get along? O God, make your name famous by revealing your mercy in their lives. Cause each of them to both show and see you in each other. For your name's sake, work in them what needs to be done to show your glory to them and to those who are looking on!

> And Lord, what about their children? Oh, I love them dearly, and I'm worried about how everything is affecting them. Lord, I'm concerned how all the chaos in their home is affecting their image of you. How can they

pray "Your kingdom come, your will be done" when their minds are so saddened by all they see and hear?

O Father, for the sake of your name and how these children see you—for the sake of your name, bring your peace and love to this home. And for the sake of your name, let neighbors, friends, and family see your grace and power at work! Amen.

God gave me a blank check when I prayed for my dear friends. I believe I filled it in well, based on the prayers we have looked at in this chapter.

God has given us a blank checks and invited us to go ahead and fill it in. But He has warned us to use it wisely. Use it for big requests, and be certain they are for things Jesus will have no trouble putting His name on.

What did we learn in this chapter?

Cats have been taught that prayer is the time to ask God to make their lives safe, soft, easy, and comfortable, and if not for them then for someone they know. Cat prayers are at worst selfish and at best shortsighted and meager. Even if Cat prayers are not self-centered, they are people centered rather than God centered. Cat concerns are temporal rather than eternal.

But when Dogs pray for God's sake and for the sake of His name, they can be bold in their prayers. They feel free to fill in the blank check with huge requests. Both Joshua and Daniel could have asked for mere happiness or relief from pain, but they weren't so shortsighted. They asked for an entire nation and for God's reputation!

Raise your sights. Raise your requests. Learn to pray in Jesus' name and make big, bold prayers! Don't be satisfied just learning to bark in prayer—learn to *howl* loud and long!

4

The Purposes of Prayer

Wе hope you now are realizing that our prayers need to be God centered—focused on His kingdom, seeking to make *Him* famous—if we want them answered.

In the previous chapter we looked at the "blank check" Jesus gives us in John 14:13; 16:23–24. We learned to be careful about how we fill out the check.

We will now look at those verses again to discover the *purposes* of prayer. We begin by asking the question, Why does God want us to intercede for others and to petition things for ourselves? We'll find answers by finishing the reading of those same two passages in John.

Praying to Bring God Glory

John 14:13 says, "Whatever you ask in My name, that will I do, *so that* . . ." (emphasis added).

Now stop right there. The words *so that* point us to something very important. Jesus is getting ready to tell His disciples why He wants to answer their prayers. Do you think he said, "Whatever you ask in My name, that will I do, *so that* you may have a safe, soft, easy, and comfortable life right where you are"? Is that what Jesus said? Absolutely not! But most Cat Christians use prayer for this purpose, unfortunately. Like real cats, they want to get from birth to death in the safest, softest, easiest, most comfortable fashion possible.

Sometimes it is very important to find out what Scripture does not say before we can realize the full impact of what it *does* say. Well then, what did Jesus say? What *is* the purpose of prayer? Let's read the verse correctly: "Whatever you ask in My name, that will I do, *so that* the Father may be glorified in the Son" (emphasis added).

There it is: Jesus wants to answer our prayers so that He can bring glory to His Father! How did we miss that before? Because of Cat Theology. Cats rarely take notice of things they think don't apply to them.

We sometimes read important words like these as if they were nothing more than spiritual fluff. But here Jesus communicates that prayer is all about glorifying the Father!

This brings us to examine our motivation to pray. Why do we come before the throne of God in petition and intercession? Is it for our sake or His sake? Is it to advance our kingdom or His kingdom? Will it make us famous or will it make Him famous? Those are the differences in the motivations of Cat and Dog Christians.

As we learned in previous chapters, if Cats pray longing to supply their selfish wants and pleasures, God answers something like, "Sorry, I'm going to say no to that prayer."

Praying to Receive Joy

We can discover a second purpose of prayer in John 16:23–24: "Truly, truly, I say to you, if you ask the Father for anything in My name, He will give it to you. Until now you have asked for nothing in My name; ask and you will receive, *so that . . .*" (emphasis added).

So that what? Why does Jesus want to answer our prayers? "*So that* your joy may be made full" (emphasis added).

What? After all this, are we back where we started? Do you mean it's about us after all? (Cats have the prospect of being very delighted at this point.)

Well, yes and no. Yes, it is about us, and not only about us having joy but having it in its fullest form. (Cats' expectations are mounting.) Joy in what? In things? In people? In accomplishment? In honor or prestige? In finances? No, because as we tie this passage with John 14:13, the meaning is clear. We find joy *in glorifying God*. Having joy in the fullest and glorifying God are intimately and intrinsically linked.

You and I should be excited when we bring our Father glory! That's what should drive us. Just as a dog is excited to see its master and that joy seems to expand and explode the more intensely they play together, our souls should explode with joy when we are enjoying our Master. We should be saying, "I get excited when my Father is glorified!"

(A side note here. If you've never experienced this, you do have something wonderful ahead of you. Admittedly, if you've never experienced this kind of joy, it might be difficult for you to understand how you can be joyful in someone else's glory. And we understand that saying you *should* do this but you don't is like saying you should enjoy chocolate ice cream when you don't. We seem to have little control over what we like. However, let our experience in this encourage you—once you do get a taste for chocolate ice cream, it's really, really good! And once you do develop a taste for joy in the glory of God, it's really, really good!)

Prayer is not calling on a celestial Santa Claus to fulfill all our wishes. As John Piper has said, it is not a "domestic intercom" for ordering our desires from our heavenly staff. It is rather like a "wartime walkie-talkie" to call for the supplies necessary to advance God's kingdom.[3] Prayer is a tool to be used to reveal God's glory in wonderful, mighty, magnificent ways.

Our Strength or God's?

Now that we know the two purposes of prayer—to glorify God and to bring us joy—let's build on this. God not only wants us to pray for things that will bring Him glory, but He also wants us to pray in a way that will bring us joy. You might ask, "Are there different ways to pray?" Yes, but we're not referring to physical positions or the words we use but to the attitude of our heart.

Here's an example to help you understand where we're going. When I (Bob) was in college, I used to type out my prayers and pray them over and over and over again: "Lord, help me to be holy. Help me to live with an eternal perspective. Help me to share my faith. Help me to hunger for your word. Help me do this, help me become that . . ."

As I was typing those words, I somehow felt the Lord say to me, "Bob, what are you asking me to do?"

And I said, "Lord, what do you mean what am I asking you to do? It is obvious. I need your help."

"Yes, Bob, but what does that mean?"

"What do you mean, 'What does it mean?' I need your help. I can't live the Christian life without you."

"Yes, but what does that mean?"

"It means, Lord, I can only do so much by myself!"

And then *boom!* I got a weighty insight. *I was trying to live a certain percentage of the Christian life all by myself,* in my own strength. I would never have thought to put a percentage on it, but my share might have been 70 percent while I asked God to put in the 30 percent I couldn't do. The point is that whatever the percentage was, I was trying to live the Christian life out of my own resources.

Now let's skip ahead to Judgment Day, when awards are being given out in heaven. Maybe it will be like going to the Olympics. There I am, standing on the highest platform, getting the gold medal, because I did the greatest percentage of the work, after all. And this leaves Jesus standing a bit lower than me, getting the silver medal. Inscribed on my gold medal is "70 percent" and in Jesus' silver medal, "30 percent." Try to picture me putting my arm around Jesus and saying, "Thanks, Jesus. I couldn't have done it without you!"

Not only is that image ludicrous, but understand this: by calling on the Lord to do only 30 percent of the work, I limited my dependence on Him—and therefore my growth—by 70 percent! My point here is not to try to reduce my actions to percentages but to say that my lack of complete dependence on the Lord did not glorify Him or bring me full joy.

Read John 15:5 to see if it says this: "I am the vine, you are the branches; he who abides in Me and I in him, he bears much fruit, for apart from Me you can only do 70 percent." Is that what the Bible says? No, it doesn't say that. Again, we're pointing out what Scripture doesn't say so we can better understand what it *does* say. And what does this verse say? "Apart from Me you can do *nothing*" (emphasis added). Nothing? Nothing!

Cats might respond with great exception, "Lord, we can

put men on the moon; we can beam our voices and videos around the globe in less than a second; we've made airplanes that can fly hundreds of miles an hour and rockets that can speed along at tens of thousands of miles per hour! We've got computers that can sort through billions of bits of information in nanoseconds; we can save premature babies from death; we can . . ."

We can do nothing. *Nothing of eternal significance.* Nothing that will last forever. Everything we do in our own strength will burn. God tells us this in 1 Corinthians 3:15: "If any man's work is burned up, he will suffer loss; but he himself will be saved, yet so as through fire."

Will we be saved? Yes. But the work we do in our own power and strength will be burned up. We will suffer loss. Bob would be suffering a 70 percent loss of potential rewards if he only depended on the Lord only 30 percent of the time. The psalmist put it this way: "Unless the LORD builds the house, they labor in vain who build it" (Psalm 127:1).

Much of Cats' lives are vain labor because Cats live mostly out of their own resources.

Cause-Me Prayers

So how can we avoid living in the power of the flesh? How do we keep ourselves from losing our heavenly rewards? How can we avoid living life as a Cat?

For the answer, we're going to look at a passage from Ezekiel 36. First, let's consider the context. God was speaking through the prophet Ezekiel about bringing the Israelites back from their time of punishment in Babylon. This judgment of exile in Babylon that God had given His people was not going to last forever. Speaking through Ezekiel, God told the people what was going to happen when the Lord restored them to the Promised Land: "Moreover, I will give you a new heart and put a new spirit within you; and I will remove the heart of stone from your flesh and give you a heart of flesh. I will put My Spirit within you and *cause you* to walk in My statutes, and you will be careful to observe My ordinances" (Ezekiel 36:26–27, emphasis added).

Did you notice two key words in verse 27? God didn't say, "I will *help you* to walk in My statutes." He said, "I will *cause you* to walk in My statutes."

There are two key reasons why God wants to do the work himself. First, the true work that needs to be done in our life is a spiritual matter. It deals with our spirit, which has been rebirthed by the Holy Spirit coming to live inside of us. By ourselves we can do nothing to bring about any spiritual growth. (This is why Jesus said that we could do *nothing* apart from Him.) Nothing that we do in our flesh—in our own power and strength—can please God: "Those who are in the flesh cannot please God" (Romans 8:8). This is where a Cat's work is "in vain" (Psalm 127:1) and will burn up (1 Corinthians 3:15).

But there is a second reason God wants to do the work himself: if we do the work ourselves, we will get the glory for it, and once again we will have robbed God of His glory! We will get the gold medal and Jesus the silver.

So Dogs learn to pray *cause-me prayers*, which sound like this:

> "Lord, cause me to be holy."
> "Cause me to live with an eternal perspective."
> "Cause me to share my faith."
> "Cause me to hunger for Your Word."

"Cause me to seek Your face."

"Cause me to thirst for righteousness."

Cause-me prayers communicate to God, "Lord, I want to be 100 percent dependent on You to work in me and through me, so that the work done in my life will last forever and You will get the glory!"

Does being 100 percent dependent on God mean we can be couch potatoes and never lift a finger toward our own spiritual growth? No! Absolutely not. We still need to give God opportunities to work in us, but we realize that unless *He* does the work, nothing of eternal significance will happen. In other words, we might pray like this:

"Lord, I'm still going to have quiet times, but unless You meet with me and open my eyes, nothing is going to happen."

"Lord, I'm still going to share my faith, but unless You speak through me, no lives will be changed."

"Lord, I'm still going to study Your Word, but unless You open my eyes, I won't learn a thing!"

"Lord, I'm going to put a filter on my computer to keep me away from pornography, but unless You fill my desire for intimacy *with Yourself*, I'll still be addicted to seeking intimacy in all the wrong places."

"Lord, I'll use all my willpower to stay away from the bar, but I feel helpless to resist the temptation of drinking unless Your Spirit quenches my thirst."

"Lord, I'm trying to resist the temptation to comfort myself with food, but I realize it won't matter how skinny my body gets unless I get "fat" on Your Word and enjoy the sweetness of You."

Our spiritual growth is contingent on our being 100 percent dependent on God. Our part is to give God times and opportunities to do His work and receive His rightful glory. David said it this way in Psalm 115:1: "Not to us, O Lord, not to us, but to Your name give glory because of Your loving-kindness, because of Your truth."

You might wonder if the words really matter. If we say, "Help me" instead of "Cause me," are we limiting our growth as Christians? Not necessarily. What matters is the attitude of our heart. Do we really believe that only God can do eternal work in us and through us?

Even as we write this, we still sometimes mix help-me prayers with cause-me prayers. But God is not worried about the words; He's concerned about the attitude of the heart—the part that distinguishes Cats from Dogs. Again, our attitude in prayer should be aimed at bringing God glory.

Commanded to Pray

As a magnifying glass can focus light intensely, we now want to focus attention on this: God not only *wants* us to pray, He *commands* us to come to Him with *all* of our problems.

Jesus *wants* you to come to Him! He invites you! "Come to Me, all who are weary and heavy-laden, and I will give you rest" (Matthew 11:28). But notice that this is not *just* an invitation; it is a command: "Come." And this is not a unique verse. There are many others. Here is one: "Call upon Me in the day of trouble; I shall rescue you, and you will honor me" (Psalm 50:15).

"But isn't that getting back to making my life safe, soft, easy, and comfortable?" you might ask. That's a good question, and it deserves a good answer. First, let's not forget that God wants us to be dependent on Him. If we didn't have needs and problems, how could we be dependent? Because this is a command, when Dogs come to God with their problems, they are honoring Him. They give Him glory. *The best way you can honor God and the best way you can glorify God is to bring Him your problems and needs.* But it must be with an attitude of laying these things at His feet rather than "Fix this for me so I can be safer and my life can be softer, easier, and more comfortable."

Why? Because when God answers those problems and needs, He gets the glory He rightfully deserves, and then we get our greatest joy! Giving God the greatest glory also gives us our greatest joy. These two goals are inseparably related to each other!

But does God mean *every* problem? Yes. Every one of them. You might wonder if God will get tired of you coming to Him with all your problems, since you have so many. No, God won't get tired of you. And why? Because the more you come to Him, the more glory He gets, and the more joy you get in seeing His provision as He answers. God never tires of revealing His glory and giving you joy!

Remember, prayer is about God's glory being revealed and our joy becoming full!

With this kind of attitude, we can now realize that when we stand at the heavenly Olympics and the medals are given out, Jesus will be standing on the main platform with no one else around. He will be receiving the gold medal inscribed "100 percent," and no one else will claim any part of the prize. No silver or bronze medals will be awarded.

It's with this picture in mind that we can better understand God's declaration that He will not give His glory to another (Isaiah 42:8), and Paul's insight when he said, "Now to our God and Father be the glory forever and ever" (Philippians

4:20). Are your prayers being answered? Do you want your prayers answered? Do you want a joy that is full? Then pray in such a way that it will glorify God.

What did we learn in this chapter?

We looked at what prayer is *not* about. Prayer is not about living like a Cat, seeking to get from birth to death in a safe, soft, easy, and comfortable manner. This is how most Christians abuse prayer and, as a result, don't get their prayers answered.

Instead, prayer is about glorifying God in two ways. First, we glorify God by praying about His kingdom, by our dependence on Him, and by coming to Him with *all* of our problems. And second, we glorify God when our joy is full as we see His provision and answers to our prayers.

5

Don't Bless Me Like That!

S cripture has already revealed to us two primary purposes for prayer—to glorify God and to make our joy full. As we pray *cause-me* prayers and as we come to God with all our problems, God is glorified and we have more joy. This process results not only in more prayers being answered but in God *blessing* us.

God said He would bless Abraham and his descendants (Genesis 12:2), and by faith we in the church are descendants of Abraham (Romans 4:16; Galatians 3:7). What does it mean to be blessed by God? What did God mean when He said, "I will bless you"? What is happening when a child kneels beside a bed and prays, "God bless Mommy, God bless Daddy, and God bless Grandma and Grandpa"? What does God hear? What is He thinking?

Just about everybody asks God at one time or another to bless someone or themselves, and there is absolutely nothing wrong with that. But remember, as with other kinds of prayers, we can pray selfish, Catlike prayers for blessing ("Lord, bless me with this; bless me with that"), or we can pray like unselfish Dogs ("Lord, bless me so I can glorify Your name in this way").

In this chapter we are going to look at how God desires to bless us. We want to help you understand that God is already answering many of your prayers for blessings and you may not even realize it, because His blessings can come in unexpected ways. Ephesians 3:20 says, "Now to Him who is able to do far more abundantly beyond all that we ask or think . . ." Beyond what we can ask or think? Indeed. God can bless us in ways and means we've never imagined! (This excites the greedy nature of Cats, but it draws awe in the heart of Dogs.)

In the Old Testament the Hebrew word for *blessing* is the word *barak*, which occurs 332 times. *Barak* is derived from a noun that means "knee" and perhaps suggests the bending of the knee in prayer. Picture a knight kneeling before his king, who taps the knight with a sword to bestow blessing and honor on him. God's blessings come to us in many forms, including success, prosperity, and longevity (things that Cats love to ask for!). These blessings are for us to enjoy, but they also make God look good. How? Let's go back to the knight kneeling before his king.

The knight's position shows subservience to the king even as the king honors the knight! As you bend your knee to God in prayer, you are honoring Him by demonstrating your subservience to Him. (This is a Dog's heart!) In other words, as God blesses us, we get to honor Him and reveal His glory.

Blessing in the Old Testament

Let's see two different ways the relationship between God's blessings and His glory was lived out in the Old Testament.

How God Blessed Jacob

First, let's consider Jacob, whom God blessed on three specific occasions. In these three instances, the words used for *blessed* are forms of *barak*:

- In Genesis 27, Jacob's father, Isaac, blessed him (with the blessing due a firstborn son, which should have gone to Jacob's brother, Esau).
- In Genesis 28, God repeated to Jacob the promises of blessing He had given to Abraham, because Jacob was part of Abraham's seed.
- In Genesis 32, Jacob wrestled with God until he received God's blessing.

So what did Jacob's life look like, having been triply blessed? To be honest, not all that great!

Because he had lied to his father to steal his brother's blessing, Jacob left home in fear for his life. He traveled to Paddan Aram, where his mother's relatives lived. After working hard to marry his uncle Laban's daughter Rachel, whom he loved, Jacob was tricked on his wedding night when Laban gave him Rachel's sister Leah instead.

Seven years later Jacob married Rachel also, but then he had two wives who constantly bickered and competed with each other through their children.

Laban cheated Jacob of his wages multiple times.

Years later, Jacob and his family left Laban and started on the long journey home. He still feared encountering his brother, thinking that his brother would kill him for stealing the blessing so many years before.

He wrestled with God, who dislocated his hip, and he walked with a limp the rest of his life.

This record alone might be more than enough to discourage us from wanting any type of triple blessing, but there's more!

Jacob had thirteen children, who added to the dysfunction of the family. Some of the sons plotted to kill their brother Joseph (because Jacob favored him), but instead they sold Joseph as a slave to a passing caravan. The brothers then conspired to lie to Jacob about what had happened, and they kept up the lie for the next twenty years. Finally, toward the end of his life, Jacob learned that Joseph was alive and well in Egypt, and he went to live there.

Jacob summed up his life like this: "The years of my sojourning are one hundred and thirty; few and unpleasant have been the years of my life" (Genesis 47:9). That's right. That was Jacob's outlook—"I've had an unpleasant life."

The actual Hebrew word for *unpleasant* is the word *ra*, which means "evil." So Jacob, in rehearsing his life story, summarized it, "My life has been evil." Jacob and his entire family could have benefited from some intense, long-term, biblical counseling! Yet he had been three times blessed by God! Obviously, the blessing that Jacob received was not the abundant life Cat Christians are looking for today.

So just how was Jacob blessed by God?

Think about two things: first, one of the definitions of being blessed is "to be successful"; second, one purpose of prayer is to reveal God's glory. Therefore, because Jacob was triply blessed, we can assume he was very successful at revealing God's glory, or making God famous.

Did Jacob make God famous? Absolutely yes! From Genesis on, the Almighty referred to himself as the God of Abraham, Isaac, and Jacob. Jacob made God extremely famous, and God used him to help start a nation. Jacob (whose new name from God was Israel) led his family to the country of Egypt, where the children of Israel were put into safekeeping for four hundred years. And at the conclusion of the four hundred years, God would make a name for himself that endures to this day!

God blessed Jacob exceedingly by making him a key player in a chain of events that led to significantly establishing God's reputation. Yet Jacob felt his days were "unpleasant," or "evil." Why? Maybe Jacob was looking at his life through Cat eyes.

Realize that if you ask God to bless you, your days may be "unpleasant"; bad things may happen to you. That could be God's blessing in your life! While Cats abhor this, Dogs are exceptionally grateful to be used by God, even if it means hardship or death.

God could be looking at you and saying, "I'm going to answer your prayer by giving you an opportunity to make me famous. I'm going to allow tough times in your life, and as you walk through them with your eyes on me, you'll be making me famous in others' eyes!" To this a Cat Christian might say, "No thanks, that's not what I signed up for!"

How God Blessed Joseph

Now let's look at Joseph, who was Jacob's favorite son. He too was greatly blessed and successful. In fact, the Bible says, "The LORD was with Joseph, so he became a successful man" (Genesis 39:2). A Cat Christian might desire to be successful too. But remember, Joseph was sold by his brothers into slavery, where he suffered physically and emotionally:

- He couldn't go back home.
- He wasn't allowed to own anything, not even the clothes on his back.
- He had no house.
- He had no family.
- He owned no camels.
- He had no sheep.
- He served at someone else's beckoning.
- In fact, everything he touched belonged to someone else.

Yes, Scripture tells us Joseph was successful, but not with the success the world speaks of today. Joseph was successful and blessed in how God used him to bring glory to His name and to fulfill His purposes. Joseph made God famous. He revealed and reflected God's glory.

As a slave in Egypt, Joseph labored hard to make another man rich. Because of Joseph, God blessed the household of Joseph's Egyptian master—a Gentile (someone who wasn't from God's chosen people). As the Lord's blessing on Joseph caused Potiphar's household to thrive, Potiphar entrusted everything to Joseph's care (Genesis 39:3–5).

We need to understand that when we ask God to bless us, we may find ourselves working hard at a job and doing good work just to make some non-Christian rich and successful. We might see this as a curse, but only if we aren't looking at it through God's eyes—if we are still expecting prayer to be about making our life safe, soft, easy, and comfortable. But God looks at it differently and says, "No, you are making me look good. This *is* my way of blessing you. I am with you as you work, and others will see me in you."

Long before Joseph was elevated to be the second in

command of Egypt (now that's the kind of blessing we like!),
he was still greatly blessed by God even though he didn't own
a thing.

A life lesson for Cats: be aware that being blessed may
show itself in unexpected ways, including some that may not
be safe, soft, easy, or comfortable but also show the undeni-
able fingerprints of God.

Blessing in the New Testament

What does the New Testament have to say about blessing? There are six different Greek words used for *blessing*
in the New Testament, and each has various forms. The one
that focuses the most on people being blessed is *makarios*,
which is used about fifty times. The root idea of *makarios*
is this: being so satisfied with God that no matter what the
circumstances might be, we still have peace and joy.

Let's repeat that, because you might need time for it to
sink in. The New Testament word most used to designate being blessed has to do with being so satisfied with God that no
matter what the circumstances might be, we still have peace
and joy.

This is why Jesus could say, "Blessed [*makarios*] are
the gentle, for they shall inherit the earth. . . . Blessed [*makarios*] are those who have been persecuted for the sake of
righteousness, for theirs is the kingdom of heaven. . . . Blessed
[*makarios*] are you when people insult you and persecute
you, and falsely say all kinds of evil against you because of
Me. Rejoice and be glad, for your reward in heaven is great"
(Matthew 5:5, 10–12).

When we have God-derived peace and joy in the midst of
difficult circumstances, others become curious to know about

the God who gives that peace and joy. This really makes God look good! It makes Him famous!

Even though God's blessings can come in different forms — and some may be adverse — a Dog can still be content!

How God Blessed Stephen

Let's look at an example of this from the New Testament.

Have you ever received a standing ovation? Maybe you spoke at a retreat or performed well at a sporting event. Would you call that standing ovation a blessing? Maybe yes, maybe no, depending on the crowd or the situation. But if God were to give you a standing ovation, would you consider *that* a blessing? Of course you would. Absolutely! Let's look at the only man in the Bible who received just that.

His name was Stephen. After the church began, he'd been chosen by the apostles to serve tables and care for widows — not a high and lofty job, but Stephen was faithful at this simple task. He was full of God's grace and power and did many miraculous signs and wonders among the people (Acts 6:8). Those who couldn't resist his wisdom used lies and physical force to get rid of him. As a result, Stephen was sentenced to death by stoning.

While being martyred for the faith, Stephen said, "Behold, I see the heavens opened up and the Son of Man standing at the right hand of God" (Acts 7:56). Stephen saw Jesus give him a standing ovation and a personal welcome into the kingdom — even while he was in his final death throes. Was Stephen at peace? Yes! "Then falling on his knees, he cried out with a loud voice, 'Lord, do not hold this sin against them!'" (Acts 7:60).

Those words testify of a man at peace and greatly blessed

by God. Stephen was content in spite of the horrible thing happening to him.

Cats need to be aware that when they ask God to bless them, God might allow them to be persecuted. They might be made fun of at the office or at school; they might be insulted because of their faith; they might be mocked or have evil things said about them.

When this happens, Cats become confused and wonder why God allowed it. Be mindful: this might be the very answer to your "God bless me" prayer! God sometimes allows our enemies and oppressors access to us so that we can reveal His glory through what is happening.

Dogs go through these difficulties with joy. As they do, they are giving glory to God, making God famous and pointing to Him as being worthy. Some people will look at these Dogs and think, *I want what that person has. I want that kind of relationship with God.*

How God Blessed Paul

Let's look at another example from the New Testament, this time the apostle Paul.

Before his conversion, Paul might well have asked God to bless him by allowing him to capture Christians, because he thought they were blaspheming God. That's when God blinded him and later revealed His plans for blessing him— Paul's blessed life was going to be about suffering for the kingdom: "He is a chosen instrument of Mine, to bear My name before the Gentiles and kings and the sons of Israel; for I will show him how much he must suffer for My name's sake" (Acts 9:15–16).

In 2 Corinthians 11:23–28, Paul recounted some of the

things he suffered for the gospel:

> Are they servants of Christ? (I am out of my mind to talk like this.) I am more. I have worked much harder, been in prison more frequently, been flogged more severely, and been exposed to death again and again. Five times I received from the Jews the forty lashes minus one. Three times I was beaten with rods, once I was stoned, three times I was shipwrecked, I spent a night and a day in the open sea, I have been constantly on the move. I have been in danger from rivers, in danger from bandits, in danger from my own countrymen, in danger from Gentiles; in danger in the city, in danger in the country, in danger at sea; and in danger from false brothers. I have labored and toiled and have often gone without sleep; I have known hunger and thirst and have often gone without food; I have been cold and naked. (NIV)

How do Cats look at Paul's life? They say, "And this man was blessed by God?"

Absolutely. Paul honored God and made God famous. God honored Paul by choosing him to write much of the New Testament and by giving him doctrinal insights that have guided the church for two millennia.

Remember the Dog's definition of blessing in the New Testament: being so satisfied with God that no matter what the circumstances may be, we still have peace and joy. Did Paul and others who suffered for the gospel have that kind of peace and joy? Yes. Scripture is clear on this. After Paul and Silas were arrested for preaching the gospel, for example, they were stripped, beaten, flogged, thrown into prison, and put into stocks. And then the Scripture says, "About midnight Paul and Silas were praying and singing hymns of praise to God, and the prisoners were listening to them" (Acts 16:25).

Paul wrote to the Philippians: "I have learned how to be content with whatever I have. I know how to live on almost nothing or with everything. I have learned the secret of living in every situation, whether it is with a full stomach or empty, with plenty or little" (Philippians 4:11–12 NLT).

Trials and Blessings

We've seen that when we pray "God bless me," God has a multitude of ways and means by which He can answer our prayer. It's not all wrapped up in the safe, soft, easy, and comfortable way we usually expect. In fact, most of those people from both the Old and New Testaments that we think of as being blessed had to undergo some tremendously difficult times:

- Abraham was blessed, but he still didn't personally receive the land promised to him. It was given to his descendants, but not until after four hundred years had passed.
- Noah was blessed, but he still had to go through the flood and the aftermath of it.
- David was blessed, but he still had countless life-and-death-situations where he confronted lions, bears, Goliath, Saul, and enemy armies, all trying to kill him.
- Daniel was blessed, but he still had to face the lions in their den, all night long.
- Shadrach, Meshach, and Abednego were blessed, but

they still had to go through the fire.

- Peter was blessed, but he still was crucified upside down.
- Paul and Silas were blessed, but they still experienced flogging and being put in stocks in prison.

Two things might be happening in the minds and hearts of Cats right now. They might look at the list above and decide they can't consider those lives as blessed because suffering doesn't fit into their definition. Or, they might realize that they've never really considered the price these people had to pay for their blessing, because Cats' memories easily forget the bad that might be attached to the good.

Look at these passages from both the Old and New Testaments (NIV) which speak of God's blessings:

"Blessed is the man whom God corrects" (Job 5:17). Has someone lovingly rebuked you recently? Did it humble you? Did it make you more like God? I'll bet you've been asking God to bless you, because you just got blessed!

"Blessed is the man who listens to me" (Proverbs 8:34). Are you listening to God? Can you understand things from His word? Then you are blessed by God.

"Blessed is he who is kind to the needy" (Proverbs 14:21). Have you recently helped someone who is poor? Did you have to spend money to help them in some way? You must have been praying, "God bless me, please."

"Blessed are all who wait for him!" (Isaiah 30:18). Are you in a waiting mode with God? Are you waiting for God, possibly feeling like He has taken a vacation from you and you are solely walking by faith? Hey, I bet you prayed, "Lord, please bless me" today. God is answering your prayers. If you are waiting for Him, God's Word says you are blessed.

"Blessed is the man who fears the LORD, who finds great delight in his commands" (Psalm 112:1). Do you fear (reverence) God? Do you delight in His commands? You have been blessed by Almighty God. Rejoice! You might not be rich. You might not have many things. But you are blessed!

"The LORD gives strength to his people; the LORD blesses his people with peace" (Psalm 29:11). Do you have strength? Do you have peace? Then you have been blessed.

"Blessed is the man who perseveres under trial" (James 1:12). Are you persevering under trial? You are blessed! Note that the trial doesn't go away. The blessing is in persevering, not in escaping from the trial!

And let's not forget the Beatitudes in Matthew 5. You can be blessed:

- When you are poor in spirit.
- When you mourn.
- When you are meek.
- When you hunger and thirst for righteousness.
- When you are merciful.
- When you are pure in heart.
- When you are a peacemaker.
- When you are persecuted.
- When people insult you and lie about you.

To Cats these do not seem like blessings, but God knows that they are. When we endure all these things with joy, we honor God, and that's what life is all about! That is success! That *is* a blessing!

Being blessed is not necessarily about acquiring things. Sometimes our having things makes God look good and gracious, but suffering and martyrdom for His name also honor Him. Consider modern believers like Corrie ten Boom (who suffered through Nazi concentration camps and lost her whole family), Joni Erickson-Tada (who became paralyzed as a teenager), and Cassie Bernall (who was shot and killed in the Columbine High School incident). Each one left a testimony that glorified God.

So when we ask God to bless us, at the heart of it we should be saying, "God, fill me with joy no matter what circumstances come our way, and through that may we make you famous. Give us the honor and blessing of having people look at our life and seeing you. We bow the knee to you. We want to be blessed by you and for you."

What did we learn in this chapter?

We saw that Cats need to understand that even if their bless-me prayers are answered, that is no guarantee their circumstances will be pleasant or prosperous, at least not in the way they've previously understood. When Cats focus on the comfortable life and narrow their vision of living for God, they actually limit His blessing.

Dogs understand that the closer they get to God—the more He is their focal point and the more they desire Him—the less meaningful it is for their lives to be preoccupied with achieving that which is safe, soft, easy, and comfortable.

Is that your testimony—or do you hear a little meow somewhere?

6

Beware and Be Aware in Prayer

In the previous chapter, we saw that God can bless us in ways we don't normally expect. God could be actively working in our life, answering our prayers right now, and we might be unaware of it. Cat Christians can be blind to how God actually is blessing them.

In this chapter we want to discuss the importance of being careful about what we ask God to give us (we call this *beware*) and being aware of our heart's true desire and how God's answer might affect us (we refer to this as *be aware*).

At this point in the book, you might be thinking, *I've learned that prayer is all about glorifying God. But the Bible says that God wants us to enjoy the things of this world: "God . . . richly supplies us with all things to enjoy" (1 Timothy 6:17). So is it OK to ask God to bless me with things I can enjoy that don't have to do with advancing God's kingdom? Is there anything in the Bible that says God will bless me with those things when I am delighting primarily in Him and not those things?*

Let us respond by saying the Bible is clear that God

"rewards those who earnestly seek him" (Hebrews 11:6 NIV), but this doesn't mean He promises them—or anyone—great health and great wealth. He might give these gifts, but He's not obligated to do so.

There is no promise of riches to Cats who are primarily seeking them. Instead, God promises to reward Dogs, that is, those who seek *Him*. In fact, it seems that most great temporal blessings in the Bible were given to those who were not directly seeking them. The Old Testament has examples of God giving people great riches in the world's eyes. He did this for Abraham, David, Solomon, and Jabez, among others, and He might do it for you. But there are also other very interesting examples that we want to review with you, to help you to *beware* and *be aware* in prayer.

There is a joke about a man and his wife in their sixties who were celebrating their fortieth wedding anniversary. On their special day a good fairy came to them and said that because they had been such a devoted couple, she would grant each of them a very special wish. The wife wished for a trip around the world with her husband. Whoosh! Immediately, she had airline and cruise tickets in her hands. The man wished for a female companion thirty years younger. Whoosh! He turned ninety! Gotta love that fairy!

The joke has a good lesson in it: God can answer our prayer the way we ask, but He doesn't always give us exactly what we intended by our request. In fact, there are examples in the Bible of God giving his children answers to prayers that flip-flopped on them and became a snare. We're going to look at three specific examples of this to discover what lessons we can learn, so that we can pray confidently and in accordance with 1 Timothy 6:17 about those things that God provides for us to enjoy.

Be Careful What You Ask For

Our first text comes from the Old Testament and is found in Numbers 11. In the desert on their journey to the Promised Land, the Israelites had already seen God miraculously provide water from a rock twice and manna for food every day. For a very brief time, they even had quail for meat.

After a year of eating only manna, even though they were close to crossing over into the Promised Land, the people started complaining, saying they would rather go back to Egypt and be slaves again. Numbers 11:4 says, "The rabble who were among them had greedy desires." (The "rabble" were Egyptians who had joined the exodus with the Israelites.)

Manna wasn't good enough for these people. They wanted more. Even though they had seen the ten plagues and the Red Sea parted, even though they had walked through the sea on dry ground, and even though they had seen the entire Egyptian army drowned when God closed the water back over them, they were not satisfied with God's provision.

Cats always want more. In spite of all that God had done and provided, the rabble were still greedy for more things.

Not only the rabble were greedy for more, but God's own believing people also joined the complaining chorus, weeping, "Who will give us meat to eat?" (Numbers 11:4). This was like saying, "God, we're not happy with where you have us in life right now. Your will for us is not good enough. We want more." They were supernaturally surviving in hostile conditions, but Cats aren't happy with merely surviving. The Israelites wanted to go beyond survival. They wanted the extras life might have to offer them.

(If you are wanting that big screen TV, luxury car, second home, or big boat, ask yourself some questions: Is it because I am listening to the greed of others around me? Why am I not satisfied with what God has already given me? Do I simply want to have the extras because my friends have them? Is it a case of "I want what I want when I want it"?)

Did the Israelites not remember their life in Egypt? Of course they did. They said so: "We remember the fish which we used to eat free in Egypt, the cucumbers and the melons and the leeks and the onions and the garlic, but now our appetite is gone. There is nothing at all to look at except this manna" (Numbers 11:5–6). Yes, they remembered all the good things they had in Egypt, but as Cats they had forgotten the oppression they suffered there as slaves. Cats have selective memory that makes it easy to focus on the joys of that nicer car, that second home, that boat and *not* on the extra maintenance, the extra payments, the insurance, the liability, and more that come right along with them. Here is a Cat lesson to be learned: it easy to forget the bad memories when you're focused only on the good stuff you don't have. This was a good time for the Israelites to remember that the good they were missing only came with the bad they had forgotten!

So did God give the Israelites meat? Did He answer their prayer or simply tell them to quit complaining? God responded through Moses: "Consecrate yourselves for tomorrow, and you shall eat meat; for you have wept in the ears of the LORD, saying, 'Oh that someone would give us meat to eat! For we were well-off in Egypt.' Therefore the LORD will give you meat and you shall eat. You shall eat, not one day, nor two days, nor five days, nor ten days, nor twenty days, but a whole month" (vv. 18–20).

Wow, this sounds like one of those above-and-beyond answers to prayer. Cats get excited when they hear answers

like this! They might think, *I'm not only going to get one boat,*
I'm going to get two or three boats! I'm not only going to get
a second house, I might end up with several houses in various
parts of the country! This is wonderful. God really does want
to bless me like He blessed Abraham, David, and Solomon!

But this "blessing" of meat for the Israelites was intended
to be a curse. Let's continue looking at the text. God said the
people would eat meat for a whole month, "until it comes
out of your nostrils and becomes loathsome to you" (v. 20).
What? God is going to give meat to them and keep giving it
to them until they gag on it and turn from it in disgust? Yes.
That's what the Bible says. Why would God do that? Moses
again: "Because you have rejected the LORD who is among
you and have wept before Him, saying, 'Why did we ever
leave Egypt?'" (v. 20).

How did the Israelites reject the Lord by simply asking for
meat? Well, they *weren't* simply asking for meat. Remember,
God doesn't listen only to words; He knows the intent of the
heart. When we're shown the Israelites' heart attitude, God's
response becomes more clear. Psalm 78:18–19 tells us that the
Israelites willfully put God to the test by demanding this food.
When their hearts are exposed, we see what God saw. They
weren't humbly asking; they were demanding. They were
testing God. Even though they had seen all the miracles of
Egypt and the exodus, they were demanding more and more
from their gracious God out of evil hearts that were never
satisfied.

God saw that their complaint was really a rejection of
Him. This is why we need to *be aware* of our heart condition
when we pray. And since we have a way of hiding the truth
from ourselves, extra care and attention should be given to our

heart condition. Just as heart attacks can come on suddenly and without warning, so can "Cat attacks." When the heart continues to be exposed, it gets pretty ugly. First Corinthians 10:6 describes what the Israelites craved as "evil things." When we crave and lust after things because we are not satisfied with what God has given us, the Bible says this is evil in the eyes of the Lord.

What was the result after God gave the Israelites the meat they craved? "While the meat was still between their teeth, before it was chewed, the anger of the LORD was kindled against the people, and the LORD struck the people with a very severe plague. So the name of that place was called Kibroth-hattaavah, because there they buried the people who had been greedy" (Numbers 11:33–34). Because of their greed and evil hearts, many died. There's an old saying, "Be careful what you ask for—you just might get it." This is why we need to *be aware* in our prayer. The Israelites' desire for things turned into a rejection of God. In spite of having just recently walked with God through miraculous events, their Cat hearts began rejecting their merciful God.

Is it possible that we can ask God for things and end up rejecting Him? And can God give us those things today so that we too get sick of them? Absolutely. God might give you the second house but you spend so much money fixing it up that it becomes a financial curse. Or you get that boat but it causes so many problems, you wish you'd never bought it. Or you drive that nicer car, but the maintenance bills are out of this world, finally making you wish you had kept the more economical car. Or the TV isn't as wonderful as you thought, and you wish you'd spent your money on something else.

So *beware*: God might give you the blessing you asked

for, but He might attach a curse to it! Really? Absolutely! "'If you do not listen, and if you do not take it to heart to give honor to My name,' says the LORD of hosts, 'then I will send the curse upon you and *I will curse your blessings*; and indeed, I have cursed them already, because you are not taking it to heart'" (Malachi 2:2, emphasis added).

There's an old joke about a group of ladies attending a morning tea, at which time many of them began admiring Mrs. Hinklemeyer's gigantic diamond ring. As they were taking notice, Mrs. Hinklemeyer warned them not to be too envious. "After all," she said, "this ring comes with the Hinklemeyer curse." That they'd never heard of the Hinklemeyer curse was evident by the looks on their faces. So she explained with a grimace, "The Hinklemeyer curse is . . . Mr. Hinklemeyer!"

Yes, a blessing might have a curse attached to it. Cats tend to welcome it anyway . . . and Dogs want nothing to do with it.

The Israelites probably didn't see themselves as rejecting God when they asked for meat. Cats are easily forgiving of their own mistakes. And we too can ask for things and never think we are rejecting God, when in reality that's exactly what we might be doing. We have an obvious need to examine our heart. If our desire for things becomes lust and greed, we are rejecting God.

The Prodigal Son

Let's now look at our second example, from the New Testament, the parable of the prodigal son. A son comes to his father and asks for his inheritance early, and the father gives it to him. The son then leaves home and goes on his merry way.

He ends up squandering all his wealth, and in repentance he returns to his father.

You might have read this story for years and never caught the significance of what happens at the beginning. The father actually finances the son's trip away from him. By giving his son the inheritance early, the father enables his son to leave his presence.

Cats need to be very careful of what they pray for because they might be asking for something that actually takes their heart away from God. Isn't this the warning God gave to the men of Israel about marrying women from other nations, that this would turn the hearts of the men away from God? (1 Kings 11:2). Yes! And it was proven in the life of King Solomon. As he took women from many other nations, his heart turned away from God, and the land became filled with idols. That boat, that second home, that nicer car, that big screen TV—whatever it is, it might not start out being a rejection of God, but it has the potential of seducing a Cat's heart away. So *beware* in prayer. Cats should be very careful about praying for things, especially things not directly tied to advancing God's kingdom.

Now you might ask, "If God knows we are going to walk away from Him when He gives these things to us, why would He give them to us in the first place?" (Oh, now there's an idea that's been tried before—blaming God for our own faults!) The answer is simple. God is looking for Christians who can survive the blessings. Cats don't have a high survival rate. (Maybe that's why they need those proverbial nine lives!)

This is no idle chat. Look again at Malachi 2:2: "'If you do not listen, and if you do not take it to heart to give honor to My name,' says the LORD of hosts, 'then I will send the curse upon you and I will curse your blessings.'" God can curse the very thing he has blessed a Cat with. The blessing we seek from God could be the very thing He curses if we do not stay Dog hearted by remaining focused on Him and the honor due His name.

Looking Spiritual or Being Spiritual?

Our third example is found in Ezekiel 14:1–3: "Then some elders of Israel came to me [Ezekiel] and sat down before me. And the word of the LORD came to me, saying, 'Son of man, these men have set up their idols in their hearts and have put right before their faces the stumbling block of their iniquity. Should I be consulted by them at all?'" A group of leaders came to inquire of God, but their hearts were not set on following Him. The Lord knew that these elders were not at all interested in His ways. (I can almost hear the meowing from here!) These men had the "form of godliness" (coming to inquire of God), but not the heart for it.

My mind pictures a Cat putting on a Dog costume and saying, "I only wear this on Sunday." Outwardly, these elders appeared to be seeking God. They looked spiritual by going to a godly man for advice. But inwardly they wanted what every other worldly person wants: money and its power . . . Cat food—that which could make their lives safe, soft, easy, and comfortable.

Why did they bother going to the prophet? They wanted God to think they were spiritual. They wanted others to think they were spiritual. And they hoped that the prophet would agree with whatever they wanted to do. Has someone ever come to you asking for godly advice but hoping you would give the answer he or she wanted? All too often, for example, husbands and wives who are unhappy in their marriages go to counselors hoping to hear, "You should get out!" They are asking someone in authority to validate what they want to do.

This is what the Ezekiel passage shows us. Cats go to God not at all interested in what God wants them to do but asking God to bless what they want done. And what usually happens when they don't get the answer they hoped to receive? They go away disappointed but still act on what they inquired about, or they go to someone else in hopes that a second opinion will be in their favor. They keep on seeking until they find someone who agrees with their point of view. They want God to approve their plans or dreams so they can feel good about what they are doing, because after all they *are* believers.

And what does God do when we ask Him to approve what we want to see happen so we can look religious yet be idolatrous? Let's look at Ezekiel 14:4: "Therefore speak to them and tell them, 'This is what the Sovereign LORD says: When any Israelite sets up idols in his heart and puts a wicked stumbling block before his face and then goes to a prophet, I the LORD will answer him myself in keeping with his great idolatry'" (NIV).

What does it mean that God is going to answer prayers in keeping with the idolatry of the person asking? It can mean one of two things. First, God could simply not answer those prayers and will tell person to repent of his idolatry. But second, God might give Cats over to their idolatry, as He did with Israelites and as the father did with his prodigal son. God will let us have our way and allow us to think it's His way too—even though it is not. In other words, He will allow us to be blinded by our own greed.

This is what God's Word speaks of regarding God giving people over to their sin (Romans 1:24). Why would God do this? He says in Ezekiel, "I will do this to recapture the hearts of the people of Israel, who have all deserted me for their idols" (14:5 NIV). God wants to turn Cats into Dogs. As always, God wants to recapture our heart; He wants us to walk humbly with Him and enjoy Him! How does giving us over to our idolatry achieve that? Simply by having our zeal for God take us so far away that one day, like the prodigal son, we wake up in our poverty and realize how bad off we really are and come back to our Master.

We need to be so careful in prayer! If not, we can pray ourselves right out of God's presence. This is a warning to churches and church leaders too! Be careful when you vote on what to do—at that moment you have the opportunity to vote yourselves out of the will of God. This is why Scripture is adamant when it says, "We destroy arguments and every lofty opinion raised against the knowledge of God, and take every thought captive to obey Christ" (2 Corinthians 10:5 ESV).

Can we pray for the good things of life that 1 Timothy 6:17 refers to? Yes, but be careful. Be careful what you ask for. And be aware of how the answer could affect you and your heart.

Simply put, beware and be aware in prayer.

What did we learn in this chaper?

Dogs have learned to be careful what they ask for . . . to be aware and beware of what they ask for and how the answer may affect them.

Cats are only concerned about getting what they want but don't yet have.

Cats have not learned contentment with what they have; they lust greedily after what they don't have.

Cats have a "selective" memory—they find it easy to forget the bad in the past (like the Israelites who forgot they were *slaves* in Egypt) when they are focused on what they don't have in the present.

Cats do not understand that a failure to keep their mind and heart on God can result in having a curse attached to their answered prayer's blessing—that a blessing from God may result in a condition that is worse for them than before they prayed.

Dogs have learned to be careful in what they ask for—they just might get it, and it won't be what they wanted.

Cats have not learned that God may give them what they ask for, but He may also "give them over" to what they ask for—in order that He might regain them later.

7

The Timing of God's Answers

Whenwe take our cars in for mechanical work, we have no problem asking, "How long will this take?" We are tempted to ask God the same question when we submit our requests to Him—"God, when can we begin looking for your answers?"

This reminds us of a story of a nightclub that opened on the main street of a small town. Deeply disturbed by this, the only church in town set up an all-night prayer meeting and asked God to burn the club down. Within a few minutes, lightning struck the club, which burned to the ground. The club's owner sued the church, but the church denied responsibility. After hearing both sides, the judge said, "It seems that wherever the guilt may lie, the nightclub owner believes in prayer while the church doesn't!"

So far, each chapter of this book has been written to drive us to focus our prayers on God and His kingdom. But even when we do, we are often discouraged by the length of time it takes to get an answer. In this chapter, we will look at what Scripture says about the timing of God's answers to our prayers.

When Answers Come Quickly

Sometimes answers do come quickly. In Genesis 24, Abraham sent his servant to find a wife for Isaac, Abraham's son. At a well at his destination, the servant asked God that the girl He had chosen as Isaac's future wife would not only give him a drink but also offer to water his camels. Then, "before he had finished praying" (Genesis 24:15 NIV), he saw a young woman named Rebekah coming out with her water jug on her shoulder. She offered him and his camels a drink. Before the servant had even finished his prayer, the answer was right there in front of him. Rebekah did become Isaac's wife. Yes, God can answer our prayers quickly—very, very quickly.

In the New Testament, God quickly answered the church's prayers regarding Peter:

> So Peter was kept in the prison, but prayer for him was being made fervently by the church to God. . . .
>
> When Peter came to himself, he said, "Now I know for sure that the Lord has sent forth His angel and rescued me from the hand of Herod and from all that the Jewish people were expecting." And when he realized this, he went to the house of Mary, the mother of John who was also called Mark, where many were gathered together and were praying. When he knocked at the door of the gate, a servant girl named Rhoda came to answer (Acts 12:5, 11–13).

While the church was still praying for Peter's release, and in spite of not believing God would answer quickly (vv. 14–16), God sent an angel to free Peter from prison.

But do these biblical examples mean *every* prayer will be answered this fast? Let's do more studying to see what other examples we've been given in Scripture.

When We Wait

Recall the story of Joseph, sold into slavery by his brothers and then falsely accused and put into prison for years.

The king's baker and cupbearer were thrown into the same prison as Joseph. Through God's perfect timing, these men both had dreams the same night. Joseph talked to them about their dreams and then interpreted the dreams.

When the cupbearer was about to be released from prison, Joseph said to him, "Please do me a kindness by mentioning me to Pharaoh and get me out of this house" (Genesis 40:14). Now although the text doesn't say it explicitly, you can bet Joseph was on his knees praying immediately and constantly, "Oh Lord, please have the cupbearer talk to Pharaoh about me."

So how long did it take for God to cause the cupbearer to mention Joseph to Pharaoh?

> Now it happened at the end of two full years that Pharaoh had a dream. . . .
>
> Then, the chief cupbearer spoke to Pharaoh, saying, "I would make mention today of my own offenses. Pharaoh was furious with his servants, and he put me in confinement in the house of the captain of the bodyguard, both me and the chief baker. We had a dream on the same night, he and I; each of us dreamed according to the interpretation of his own dream. Now a Hebrew youth was

with us there, a servant of the captain of the bodyguard, and we related them to him, and he interpreted our dreams for us" (Genesis 41:1, 9–12).

Two years passed before the cupbearer spoke to Pharaoh about Joseph—two years before God answered Joseph's prayer while Joseph stayed in the cold, dank prison. If Joseph had been a Cat, he would have given up praying during that time, or sat around in the dungeon wondering if God didn't answer his prayer because he wasn't spiritual enough.

Sometimes God answers quickly—before we finish praying. Sometimes God answers slowly—we might even think God forgot about our prayer.

Abraham could have felt like that. If Abraham married at the age his son Isaac did, he would have been forty years old. He and Sarah could have started praying for a son about that time. When God told Abraham to leave his country and his father's house (Genesis 12:1), Abraham was seventy-five. This means thirty-five years had already gone by—thirty-five years of unanswered prayer.

Then God came to Abraham and promised him a son from his own body (Genesis 15). By this time Abraham had been living in Canaan for ten years, so he was now eighty-five. When Isaac was born, Abraham was the ripe old age of one hundred.

God is not FedEx. Not all our prayers "absolutely, positively need to be there overnight." Some answers to prayer take nearly a lifetime—or longer.

When the Israelites were slaves in Egypt, how often and fervently do you think they prayed for freedom? Probably constantly and with great intensity. And how long did God wait before he answered their prayers? In Genesis 15:13 we read that God told Abraham (then called Abram), "Know for certain that your descendants will be strangers in a land that is not theirs, where they will be enslaved and oppressed *four hundred years*" (emphasis added). Their prayers weren't answered for four hundred years! That means the people who began the prayers for deliverance didn't receive an answer even in their lifetime; neither did their children or grandchildren! (No wonder a Cat needs nine lives—it could take that long to get a prayer answered!)

Why We Wait

When it does take a lengthy time to get the answer, apparently God's immediate response and instruction to us is, "Wait."

"Why?" we might inquire.

God might be developing something in us while we wait. He might also be developing or waiting for someone else. He told Abraham the Promised Land would be his but not for four hundred years, because the sins of the Amorites, the people living in the land at the time, did not yet warrant their destruction (Genesis 15:16).

Whatever the reason—and we might never know what it is—God's requirement of us is to wait.

Cats are so keenly focused on getting an immediate answer that they hardly have time to hear why God might want them to wait. But we are going to look at six reasons why God might have us wait before we see answers to our prayers:

- God wants a relationship with you, not just recognition from you.
- God might want us to learn deep lessons, which take time to learn.

- God might be waiting for us to pray humbly.
- God might want us to learn to be persistent.
- The answer could be delayed by a battle of spiritual forces.
- The praise given to God by Dogs during the waiting brings greater glory to our heavenly Father.

Let's look at each one of these reasons separately.

Relationship, Not Just Recognition

The first reason God would have us wait is this: when God hears our prayers, He is first and foremost concerned about our relationship with Him. In Psalm 18 He tells us that He delights in us. In Zephaniah 3:17 we learn He rejoices over us with shouts of joy. In the book of John, we learn that He loved us so much that He gave His only begotten Son for us that we might spend eternity with Him.

Put in very simple terms, God loves us. And when you love someone, you want to spend time with him or her so the relationship can develop. One of the best ways God gets to spend undistracted time with us is during our moments of prayer. But if we always got quick answers to our prayers, we probably wouldn't be spending very much focused time with Him. We would soon forget that Christianity is far more about relationship than it is about getting what we want when we want it.

In her book *Praying God's Word*, Beth Moore says, "Never forget that God is far more interested in our getting to know the Deliverer than simply being delivered."[4]

Christianity is about a relationship with God more than anything else. Use your prayer time to delight in God, to get to know Him, to become friends with Him. Don't simply rush through your prayer list. God wants you to know Him intimately, not use Him to get what you want!

Deep Lessons Take Time to Learn

Here is a second reason God waits to answer many of our prayers: God sometimes has deep lessons for us that take a long time to learn. Until we've learned those deep lessons, God delays His answer.

With this in mind, how can impatient Cats begin to pray more like Dogs? Cats need to ponder what God is focused on as they pray. They might need to say, "Lord, if there are lessons I need to learn, do *not* answer my prayers until I've learned those lessons. I probably need those lessons far more than I need the answer to my prayer. You are preparing me for eternity, so I'll be patient."

Notice how this worked in Joseph's life. Joseph started out with an arrogant attitude, telling his brothers and parents that they were going to bow down to him (Genesis 37). He ended up quite humble, forgiving his brothers and resting in God's sovereignty (Genesis 50:15–21). Did this happen overnight? No. It took years for God to work in Joseph the qualities God wanted him to have.

This can be true in many lives. God might want to do things in us before He answers our prayers. Being aware of this points us to a third reason why God sometimes tells us to wait.

God Wants Us to Pray with Humility

We don't always see the big picture, whether there are lessons we or others need to learn; therefore, we need to pray humbly rather than arrogantly making demands. This might be hard to hear, but immediate answers to our prayers can be God's secondary priority for us. Instead of providing immediate answers, He might choose to slowly answer our prayer over the course of years while He is busy developing patience and character in us. As a familiar saying goes, "God is more concerned with your character than your comfort."

God wants to see humility not only in our prayers but also in our life.

When Rehoboam's kingdom was established (2 Chronicles 12), he and all Israel abandoned the law of God. God wasn't happy about this and led King Shishak of Egypt to attack Israel for their arrogance. While the leaders huddled in fear, God sent a prophet to them with the words of the Lord: "You have abandoned me, so I am abandoning you to Shishak." Rehoboam and the leaders of Israel humbled themselves and said, "The LORD is right in doing this to us!" (2 Chronicles 12:5–6 NLT). When the Lord saw their change of heart, He gave this message to the prophet: "Since the people have humbled themselves, I will not completely destroy them and will soon give them some relief" (v. 7 NLT).

Humility releases God to work in our life. Humbling ourselves before God shows itself in many different forms; one of the greatest is in the area of acknowledgment and submission. In any given situation, we might not know God's will, plans, and purposes, so Dogs submit to His timetable. This was the attitude of Shadrach, Meshach, and Abednego as they faced the fiery furnace: "If it be so, our God whom we serve is able to deliver us from the furnace of blazing fire; and He will deliver us out of your hand, O king. But even if He does not . . ." (Daniel 3:17–18). These three young men weren't absolutely certain that God would keep them from dying in the furnace—only that He could if He so chose. They were quite humble in both their attitude and prayer. This could be one of the key reasons God honored their prayer.

Humility was also the attitude of Jesus when He thought about going to the cross. It's obvious He was in turmoil; He asked that God would take away "this cup of suffering." But then he humbly said, "Yet I want your will to be done, not mine" (Luke 22:42 NLT).

Note that even though His prayer was prayed humbly, God's answer was still no. A humble prayer is what God requires, but humility does not guarantee that we get our way. God is sovereign, and His purposes and His ways are best.

To what degree would your prayer life be altered if you took up this humble attitude? Dogs should boldly come before God's throne asking Him to deliver them while at the same time saying, "Lord, I want your will to be done, not mine. I humbly ask this and submit this to your plan. I realize that what you want could be different from what I am asking for, and if that is the case, that's fine. I yield to your will."

God Wants Us to Persevere in Prayer

A fourth reason God sometimes tells us to wait is that He wants to teach us to persevere in prayer. God clearly told us that He wants us to be persistent in our prayers and not give up. Jesus gave us an example of this with the story of a widow who went before an unrighteous judge again and again, demanding her rights:

> There was a judge in a certain city . . . who neither feared God nor cared about people. A widow of that city came to him repeatedly, saying, "Give me justice in this dispute with

my enemy." The judge ignored her for a while, but finally he said to himself, "I don't fear God or care about people, but this woman is driving me crazy. I'm going to see that she gets justice, because she is wearing me out with her constant requests!"

Then the Lord said, "Learn a lesson from this unjust judge. Even he rendered a just decision in the end. So don't you think God will surely give justice to his chosen people who cry out to him day and night? Will he keep putting them off?" (Luke 18:2–7 NLT)

How does this change your prayer life? Let me tell how it changed mine (Bob).

I learned to pray what I call *LSD* prayers, for "long, steady, and disciplined." In other words, I have prayers that I have prayed consistently for thirty years. These are the same prayers I started typing in college. Prayers such as these:

"Lord, break me and make me the man of God You want me to be." (I turned fifty this year and still pray this prayer.)

"Lord, cause me to be holy. Cause me to love You."

"Lord, cause me to love my wife." (I have been praying like this for two decades.)

I pray these prayers over and over. Why? Because I can always be broken more. I can always be more holy. I can always love God more. I can always love my wife more. And I know that the answers to these prayers are going to take time, lots of time. There are no quick fixes to building godly character into a person. I've been commanded to come before God day and night, so like the widow before the judge, I keep praying these prayers.

(One reason we created Prayer To Go is to help people pray LSD prayers that will keep them patient and disciplined in coming before God. For more information on this, check it out at www.PrayerToGo.com.)

Remember that as we come before God again and again and again, we are spending more time with Him. And what is that doing? It is helping to build our relationship with Him—and Christianity is first and foremost a relationship. LSD prayers keep us dependent on God and growing in our relationship with Him.

Spiritual Battles Can Delay God's Answers

A fifth reason we might have to wait before our prayers are answered is fighting between good and evil in the spiritual realm. (Yes, there really is spiritual warfare taking place around us in a realm we do not even see.)

The Bible tells us Daniel had to wait three weeks for his answer, even though God sent the answer immediately after Daniel prayed. An angel told Daniel, "Do not be afraid, Daniel, for from the first day that you set your heart on understanding this and on humbling yourself before your God, your words were heard, and I have come in response to your words. But the prince of the kingdom of Persia was withstanding me for twenty-one days" (Daniel 10:12–13). Unseen warfare in the spiritual realm had delayed Daniel's answer to prayer for twenty-one days.

There are things happening all around us that we know nothing about. It might be God's overall plan being worked out in a way we didn't foresee, or it might be spiritual warfare raging all about us, but unseen and unfelt. Like the persistent widow coming before the judge, Dogs will be persistent and patient, knowing that an answer might be withheld due to spiritual warfare taking place in the heavens.

Praising God While We Wait Gives Him Greater Glory

The sixth reason God might have us wait for answers to prayer is so our praise for His faithfulness will be far greater. To see this, let's go back to the faith of Shadrach, Meshach, and Abednego. Their deliverance wasn't sure, but still they praised God no matter what the outcome would be for them. "If it be so, our God whom we serve is able to deliver us from the furnace of blazing fire; and He will deliver us out of your hand, O king. But even if He does not, let it be known to you, O king, that we are not going to serve your gods or worship the golden image that you have set up" (Daniel 3:17–18).

Praising God and trusting Him before the answer to prayer comes is in many ways far more glorious than after the answer comes. Cats find it easy to praise God *after* they get their request fulfilled, but Dogs persist in praise *before* they get His response—and sometimes even when they don't.

Cats focus their prayers more on gratitude than glory. Gratitude is giving thanks for something someone did for you. Glory is an attitude of thanks for who that someone is. Gratitude is based on us, glory on the character of the other person. Too often our praise is merely thanking God for what He did for us, and we spend far too little time glorifying Him for who He is.

Right now our ministry is down to bare bones financially. If God doesn't move quickly, we will be down to nothing. But our praise to God is rich and brings Him such glory. Why? Because we don't have the money yet, and we are still declaring His faithfulness. It will be easy to praise God after the money comes, but now is when the potential for glorifying God is the greatest! We believe God is having us wait. And we are at peace with that. It might not be convenient or comfortable, but we rejoice in it because our joy is in Him.

God could have you waiting simply to declare His glorious praise while you wait. Remember, for a Dog the waiting can be glorious even before an answer comes.

What did we learn in this chapter?

First, sometimes God will quickly answer our prayers, yet at other times God is very slow to answer. During the slow times, God is saying, "Wait."

When I (Gerald) go to the doctor's office, there's a usual waiting time even though I had an appointment. During that waiting time, I'm often left wondering, *What is that doctor doing? I don't see anyone coming or going. I don't hear any conversation. Is he even here?*

In that same way, without proper understanding, Cat Christians can be left wondering if God is doing anything—if He's even there, if He's even listening.

But Dogs rest assured. They know that waiting on God is a valuable lesson that many Bible characters had to learn. God could be asking you to wait. You simply need to ask one question, Is what I'm praying for about God's kingdom or my kingdom? If it is for God's kingdom, then learn to wait patiently and be at peace.

8

Why Does God Say No?

In the previous chapter we discovered that God might tell us to wait for the answers to our prayers. Why? Because there is something else He wants to do during the waiting time; it's not that He won't answer but rather that waiting will bring about something more pleasing to Him. And we looked at six reasons why God might have us wait.

In this chapter we're going to answer the question, Why is God's answer to our prayers sometimes no?

By looking at eleven prayers in the Bible that were clearly answered no and asking ourselves what can we learn from them, we've discovered four major reasons God sometimes says no: sin in our life, asking for what is outside of God's will, "no" producing a greater revelation of God's glory than "yes," and praying selfish prayers.

In this chapter we are going to look closely at these four reasons, investigating examples of the eleven prayers to see why God responded negatively. Then we'll do a quick survey of other reasons God might deny our prayer requests.

Sin in Our Life

One reason God gave a no answer to prayers in the Bible is that there was sin in the life of the one praying. One Old Testament example is Moses. After Moses brought the Israelites out of Egypt, they had to pass through the desert, where they complained multiple times to God and to Moses. Twice they complained about not having water.

On the first complaint, God told Moses to *strike* the rock with his staff, and water would come from it. Moses struck it, and water did come out. The second time, God told Moses to *speak* to the rock and water would come out. But keep reading: "Then Moses lifted up his hand and struck the rock twice with his rod; and water came forth abundantly, and the congregation and their beasts drank. But the LORD said to Moses and Aaron, 'Because you have not believed Me, to treat Me as holy in the sight of the sons of Israel, therefore you shall not bring this assembly into the land which I have given them'" (Numbers 20:11–12).

Later, as Moses reviewed his life, he reflected on this incident with these words: "I also pleaded with the LORD at that time, saying, 'O Lord GOD, You have begun to show Your servant Your greatness and Your strong hand; for what god is there in heaven or on earth who can do such works and mighty acts as Yours? Let me, I pray, cross over and see the fair land that is beyond the Jordan, that good hill country and Lebanon.' But the LORD was angry with me on your account, and would not listen to me" (Deuteronomy 3:23–26).

It was because of Moses' sin that God refused his request.

King Saul repeatedly sought the favor of men over God, and so we find that God twice denied his requests (1 Samuel 14:37; 28:6–7).

David sinned by sleeping with another man's wife and then murdering her husband when he learned she was pregnant. When the child was born and became ill, David asked God to spare the child's life. But God said no and the boy died. Why? Because of David's sin (2 Samuel 12:14–18).

King Zedekiah got no positive help from God, but in fact he was faced with the very opposite of what he asked for because of sin (Jeremiah 21:1–9).

Of the eleven prayers in the Bible that God said no to, five were denied because of sin. How then should this change our life? Should we go around inspecting every area of our life looking for sin? The answer to that question is both yes and no.

John 16:8 tells us that it is the role of the Holy Spirit to convict us of sin. If we are listening to Him, there should be ample conviction on His timetable. He knows we cannot deal with every sin all at once. We do not need to beat up on ourselves or obsessively examine every detail of our life, asking, "Is this sin? Is that sin?" God will do what He has promised and the Holy Spirit will do His job.

Yet we should humbly be asking God to show us where any sin resides in our life and humbly be ready to deal with the sin that is revealed. Why? Because the Cat part of us is calloused to sins that still linger.

The Bible warns us that we can be deceived: "Now the Holy Spirit tells us clearly that in the last times some will turn away from the true faith; they will follow deceptive spirits and teachings that come from demons. These people are hypocrites and liars, and their consciences are dead" (1 Timothy 4:1–2 NLT).

"Their consciences are dead." The problem is, they don't

know this. They don't know they are following demons and deceptive spirits. Why? They are blind to the truth. They think they are doing right . . . but they aren't. They think they are being spiritual . . . but they aren't. They think their way is the right way . . . but it isn't.

Sin in our life will inhibit the answers we want from God. And we can be deceived about the patterns of sin in our life.

If you have any questions or doubt as to whether you are sinning, please find some people who are godly and spiritually mature and ask them to give you a spiritual checkup. Allow them to ask you tough questions about any and all areas of your life. Let them probe and see if God leads to anything specific. God might want to use this process to take away any blindness from your eyes.

Praying Outside of God's Will

The second reason God answers no is that He has plans that differ from our own. Our view of what God is up to is limited or faulty. We find examples of this in the lives of Moses, Elijah, and (we assume) Jonah. All three asked God to let them die. But God said no because what they were asking was outside of His will.

The burden of caring for God's people was great; Moses felt alone under the heavy weight and asked God to let him die (Numbers 11:14–15). But Moses still had years of work to do in continuing to lead God's people to the Promised Land.

Jonah wanted to die (Jonah 4:8–11), but he was not allowed to, and we assume God wanted Jonah to know Him better before He ended Jonah's life.

Elijah wanted to die after a great victory over the prophets of Baal, a pagan god. Elijah felt alone and was being pursued by evil people (1 Kings 19:1–4). God told Elijah something like this: "I know you are tired; I know you are emotionally drained; but I still have a purpose for you. I will not answer that prayer the way you want." God had plans for Elijah's ministry to continue. Elijah still had to speak to other kings, anoint new kings, and ordain Elisha to be a leader for God's people.

In these three cases, God told his servants that His plans and purposes for them were not finished. What they were asking went against His divine intentions, and therefore He would not grant their requests.

Sometimes God says no to our prayers because what we are asking for isn't in His good plans for us. Cat Christians rarely think about the bigger picture—they tend to only relate to their world and their life. Note too that a Dog can receive a no just as much as a Cat. What a Cat or Dog asks for might not be outlandish, selfish, hedonistic, or wrong—God simply has other plans. Therefore, Dogs pray in humility, "Lord, this is what I want, but you know best. Not my will, but yours."

A Revelation of Greater Glory

The third reason God says no is that His glory will be revealed in a greater way through some other means. In other words, the glory that will be revealed by saying no is *greater than* the glory that would be revealed by answering yes. We can see this in the lives of Jesus and Paul.

Jesus said, "My Father, if it is possible, let this cup pass from Me" (Matthew 26:39). In other words, Jesus didn't want to go through the suffering before Him. But God in essence said, "No, My Son. By Your going through this, My glory will shine forever and will bring salvation to the ends of the earth.

I am not going to take this suffering away from You or You from it."

We see a similar pattern in Paul's life. A "thorn in the flesh" (2 Corinthians 12:7) was tormenting him; what it was we do not know, but Paul wanted it gone! He asked God three times to take it away, but God said no. Why? Let's allow Paul to tell us: "Three different times I begged the Lord to take it away. Each time he said, 'My grace is all you need. My power works best in weakness'" (vv. 8–9 NLT). In other words, God told Paul, "The glory I reveal by allowing this thorn in your flesh to remain is greater than the glory that would be revealed by taking it away."

This is hard for Cats to hear, because they are not living primarily for God's glory. They are living for a safe, soft, easy, and comfortable life. Dogs can accept this much more easily because they live, first and foremost, to reveal God's glory. And if that glory can shine in a greater way, even if it means hardship for them, they gladly accept it.

There will be times when God says no to our prayers because He knows His glory will be revealed in a greater way. We need to be at peace with that. And we can be—if glorifying God is what we truly live for.

Praying Selfishly

God also says no to selfish prayers. That's where we started this book.

Cat prayers advance Cat kingdoms, not God's. And God simply says no. An example of this: James and John asked Jesus if they could sit on His left and right when Jesus established His kingdom on earth (Mark 10:35–37). They were focused on themselves. Jesus told them that rewards in His kingdom would be based on humble service (vv. 41–45).

And don't you love how James and John began their request? "Teacher, we want You to do for us whatever we ask of You." You get the idea, don't you? I'll bet God could hear their meowing all the way in heaven! Unfortunately, they sounded like many who might be reading this now. "We're not going to tell You what it is, but we want You to promise You'll do it. Promise us You'll give us what we ask before You even know what it is." Like children trying to outsmart a parent, James and John tried to force Jesus to give them a positive answer. That simply doesn't work.

But imagine for a second: what if God said yes to every selfish prayer? What would that do to us?

- We would act like spoiled brats. There are not many things worse than "Brat-Cats"!
- We would want God's presents far more than His presence.
- We would be seeking God for what He could give us, not for who He is.
- We would put a premium on our comfort, not our character.
- We would pray for perfect health and incredible wealth—but end up spiritually destitute.

We would be like children concerned only about themselves and focused only on what they get out of life, with no concern for anyone else. For the same reasons that parents sometimes tell their children no, God also says no. He doesn't want us to be spoiled Brat-Cats.

Other Reasons God Says No

We've looked at examples of prayers God answered no. Now let's quickly look at other reasons found in Scripture for God's no.

Without faith nothing happens; with faith anything can happen: "Truly I say to you, if you have faith and do not doubt, you will not only do what was done to the fig tree, but even if you say to this mountain, 'Be taken up and cast into the sea,' it will happen. And all things you ask in prayer, *believing*, you will receive" (Matthew 21:21–22, emphasis added).

"Without faith it is impossible to please God" (Hebrews 11:6 NIV).

If we are clinging to secret sin, God will not hear us: "If I regard wickedness in my heart, the Lord will not hear" (Psalm 66:18). I'm reminded of Sgt. Schultz in the old television show *Hogan's Heroes*. Whenever something questionable was happening, he said, "I see nothing! I hear nothing!" That's the same way God might be responding when we hold on to secret sins.

Unworthy offerings will prevent God's answers: In Malachi 1 God said that He was displeased with the nation of Israel because they offered defiled sacrifices that were blind, lame, and sick.

A lack of honoring and fearing the Lord will cause God to "turn a deaf ear" to us: "When they cry for help, I will not answer. Though they anxiously search for me, they will not find me. For they hated knowledge and chose not to fear the LORD. They rejected my advice and paid no attention when I corrected them" (Proverbs 1:28–30 NLT).

A lack of compassion for those who need it will bring denial of our requests: "He who shuts his ear to the cry of the poor will also cry himself and not be answered" (Proverbs 21:13).

Worshiping anything other than God will cause God to answer our prayers with no: When Judah was crying out to God, the Lord said He would not listen because "your gods are as many as your cities, O Judah" (Jeremiah 11:13).

Speaking falsely, speaking wickedly, murder, and robbery will turn God away from our requests: "But your iniquities have made a separation between you and your God, and your sins have hidden His face from you so that He does not hear. For your hands are defiled with blood and your fingers with iniquity; your lips have spoken falsehood, your tongue mutters wickedness" (Isaiah 59:2–3).

Not living rightly and kindly with a wife will prevent a husband's prayers from being answered: "You husbands . . . live with your wives in an understanding way, as with someone weaker, since she is a woman; and show her honor as a fellow heir of the grace of life, so that your prayers will not be hindered" (1 Peter 3:7).

We need to also remember that God is not obligated to answer any prayers of the unrighteous other than the prayer of repentance.

This is not rocket science. It's not something deep and mysterious. If you think God is not answering your prayers, you might be violating one or more of the principles we just looked at—and this is not meant to be a complete list! God wants to be on clear speaking terms with us, but sin and violating other scriptural principles will frustrate our prayer life. God will not go against His good plans for us by giving us our way when it is not His holy way.

It would be only fitting to close this book with a prayer:

Father, we pray that You will use this book to build formidable foundations in the lives and hearts of those who read it, that they will be better prepared, with willing hearts, to seek Your kingdom, establish Your ways, and make You famous! May You be glorified in our lives and through our prayers— through those that You grant, through those to which You say wait, and even through those to which You say no.

What did we learn in this chapter?

From the example of prayers in the Bible to which God said no, we gleaned four reasons God says no: sin in our life, asking for something outside of God's will, God's "no" producing a greater revelation of His glory, and praying selfish prayers.

We also looked at a variety of other situations that Scripture teaches us will hinder our prayers.

Prayers God Can't Answer
Final Thoughts from Gerald

Prayers God can't answer are prayers that don't really make a request for God to answer or don't give Him any room to answer. These prayers haven't really been fully considered when we ask them. If that's a bit confusing, let me give a few examples of prayers I've said and heard.

Let's begin with what appears to be one of the most common prayers—the one given before eating a meal.

Prayer #1: *"Lord, bless this food."*

Is that what we really want God to do? What do we mean by that? When Jesus began to eat, He usually "gave thanks" for the food; He had a heart of gratitude for God's provision. An occasion when He "blessed" the food was when He had thousands to feed and only a few loaves and fish to do it with.

Unless there actually were thousands to be fed, how would we know if, when, or how God actually did answer such a prayer? Maybe if we thought about it, we'd pray in gratitude (thankfulness) rather than asking God to transcend heaven and earth and upset the law of physics to do something miraculous with our sandwich.

Prayer #2: "Bless this food to the nourishment of our bodies."

I can only imagine God saying, "That was the idea I had in mind for your food all along. That's what I made it for. Are you expecting Me to do something with your hamburger that I'm not already doing or something different from what I'll do for the unbeliever who eats without being grateful?" Think about it—God made the meat, the lettuce, the pickle, and more *for* our nourishment, so what are we asking with this prayer? And how would you recognize God's answer if He did?

Prayer #3: "Lord, for what we are about to receive, make us truly thankful."

"Make us truly thankful"? Are we really such ingrates that we're not thankful already for what God provided? Do we now have to pause and ask Him to make us thankful too? Is God supposed to answer a prayer like that? Or should He just groan when He hears us ask that one?

Prayer #4: "Lord, be with Billy today."

Didn't God say He would be with us until the end of the age? Didn't He say He would never leave us? What does this prayer really intend for God to do? How is He supposed to answer if He already has?

Prayer #5: "Lord, we remember Aunt Clara at this time."

In my imagination I can hear God pondering this prayer, "You remember Aunt Clara? So do I! Now that we both remember her, is there something you wanted to ask Me?"

You might be taking exception here and say, "I think you're getting pretty picky here, Preacher." That might be true, but maybe we could give more time and consideration to praying more specifically, more strategically, more thoughtfully.

The more specific our prayer is—the better thought out it is—the more easily we could see God display His response. And the time it takes to think it through can be used as a time to become more and more acquainted with God; this is valuable time spent with Him.

Remember, God is more concerned about our relationship with Him than He is in providing a rapid response to our every query. Take time with Him . . . and learn to enjoy Him.

Putting the "Super" in Supernatural
Final Thoughts from Bob

Seeking to live like a Dog, I constantly try to keep asking, "What does God get out of this?" And the more I have tried to think this way, the more I wonder if I sometimes put God in a predicament over how to answer my prayers because of how I pray.

Take, for example, the prayers I have for my ministry. I keep asking the Lord to make the ministry of UnveilinGLORY supernatural. I pray this because I want Him to get all of the credit and glory for what happens. At the same time, I also pray that God will give us the finances that I think we need to make this ministry advance.

Currently, He is not answering these prayers the way I think He should; we don't have the money I think we need. But the ministry is growing in leaps and bounds, largely overseas. This is primarily because our international director keeps using the little money that he has to take trips that spread the message of God's glory. Because the ministry has been growing with so little money, many would say the growth is happening supernaturally.

So I wonder if God has been sitting in heaven saying to himself, *OK, he wants it to be supernatural, yet he wants more money. If I give him more money, the growth of the ministry will seem less supernatural. So I'm going to have to make a decision here. I think I am not going to give him the money he is praying for so that the ministry can be seen as more supernatural than ever!*

In essence, my prayers contradicted themselves. I want the ministry to be supernatural, yet I want money, which will make the work seem less supernatural. Now, could God provide money supernaturally through a gift of some kind to keep it all looking supernatural? Yes, but God hasn't chosen to answer in that way. That's His choice, and I need to be OK with that.

I see this contradiction in other areas of my prayer life as well.

I have been praying for over thirty years, "Lord, break me and make me the man that you want me to be." Each time I pray that prayer, I am reminded of a child breaking a pencil between his fingers while snapping it down on his leg. I really want to be broken before God. Yet at the same time, God brings opportunities into my life to break me that I'm not really wild about.

Recently, the daughter of one of my out-of-state friends had a crisis. My friend and his wife were trying to get to their daughter to be with her through this ordeal, but they were not going to be able to be here for another twenty-four hours. Because this was a major crisis, my friend called and asked if my wife and I would drive down to his daughter's place and minister to her for the night.

My friend's daughter lived over an hour away. And when I got the phone call, I had just laid down to take a nap! (I was exhausted from the day's activities.) I silently prayed, *Oh Lord, do I really have to go?*

Again, I put God in a predicament. I can only imagine Him saying, "There goes Sjogren again. He says he wants to be broken. But when I bring him those opportunities that are going to shape his life, he asks to get out of them. Which prayer am I going to answer?"

He chose to answer the "pencil prayer," and I am better for it. And not only do I want to be broken, but I've also asked the Lord to do something even deeper in my character.

My wife is generally very healthy, but recently she hurt her back. She couldn't bend down to get things; she couldn't lift anything heavy; she even needed help getting out of a chair. As much as I prayed for quick healing, the healing came slowly. And I wonder if that took place because my prayers were again contradicting each other.

You see, not only have I been praying that God would break me, I have been asking God to give me a servant's heart. And I believe God has used Debby's back problems as part of answering those prayers.

Again, I imagine God up in heaven saying, "OK, you've asked Me to give you a servant's heart. Here is your perfect chance. You get to serve your wife. You can do this by getting her the ice pack for her back and then catering to her needs. Then you get to help her out of the chair when she wants up. You can pick up things she drops. And when your family needs groceries, you can take her to the store and begin by helping her into the car and then out of the car once you get there. Then you can walk with her to find the food, put it into the cart, pull it all out for the cashier, put it back into the cart and then into the car, and then help Debby get back into the car. Once you're home, you again get to help her out of the car, get the groceries from the car into the kitchen; then you can put it all away, get her the ice bag, and then cater to her needs as she'll be wiped out on the couch again. *And you want Me to heal quickly! Do you want your prayers answered or not?"*

I had put God into a bind. Which prayer was He going to answer?

This helps me understand how God answers some prayers and not others. There are times when God is answering the "Lord, please break me" prayers. And there are times when God is going to give us the abundant, seemingly easy life.

By bringing circumstances into our life that are going to break us or make us better servants in the long run, we are going to end up becoming more like Him, radiating His glory better, and having a more abundant life. But to reach that goal, we are going to have to go through pruning times. And those times of pruning might go against other prayers we are praying!

When times are getting tough on you, when things look like they are all going downhill, when you think God has abandoned you or isn't answering any of your prayers, don't give up hope. He is involved in your life far more than you realize, but He might not be answering your prayer for an easy, safe, soft life. He could be answering the "Lord, I want to become more like You" prayers that you have prayed in years past and that will end up radiating and reflecting His glory in a greater way—though they seem to contradict what you are currently praying!

Trust in God. He has your best in mind, perfectly combined with revealing His glory in wonderful, magnificent ways.

Notes

1. Rick Warren, *The Purpose Driven Life: What on Earth Am I Here For?* (Grand Rapids: Zondervan, 2002), 17.

2. Giles Wilson, "Does Prayer Work?" *BBC News Online*, February 27, 2002, http://news.bbc.co.uk/1/hi/uk/1844076.stm (accessed April 15, 2010).

3. John Piper, *Let the Nations Be Glad*, 3rd ed. (Grand Rapids, MI: Baker Academic, 2010), 65, 69.

4. Beth Moore, *Praying God's Word: Breaking Free from Spiritual Strongholds* (Nashville: B&H Publishing Group, 2009), 128.

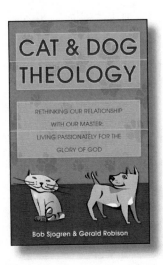

CAT & DOG THEOLOGY

RETHINKING OUR RELATIONSHIP
WITH OUR MASTER:
LIVING PASSIONATELY FOR THE
GLORY OF GOD

Bob Sjogren & Gerald Robison

There is a joke about cats and dogs that conveys their differences perfectly. A dog says, "You pet me, you feed me, you shelter me, you love me; you must be God!" A cat says, "You pet me, you feed me, you shelter me, you love me; I must be God!"

This book challenges the reader's understanding of their relationship with God. Our understanding of how we relate to God may not be wrong, but it may be incomplete. The God-given traits of cats ("you exist to serve me") and dogs ("I exist to serve you") can be similar to certain theological attitudes held by many Christians. In our personal theologies, some attitudes may draw us closer to God, and others can also pull us away from Him. This book will help the reader differentiate those attitudes, and, as a result, draw closer to the God who delights in them!

Retail: $16.00
ISBN: 978-0-8308-5621-3

Available at ivpress.com or through your local bookstore.